A GEOGRAPHY OF BLOOD

Unearthing Memory

from a Prairie Landscape

CANDACE SAVAGE

A GEOGRAPHY OF BLOOD

David Suzuki Foundation

GREYSTONE BOOKS

Vancouver / Toronto / Berkeley

Greystone Books Ltd.
greystonebooks.com

David Suzuki Foundation
davidsuzukiinstitute.org

Cataloguing data available from Library and Archives Canada
ISBN 978-1-77100-321-6 (pbk.)
ISBN 978-1-926812-69-4 (ebook)

Editing by Nancy Flight
Copyediting by Shirarose Wilensky
Jacket and text design by Naomi MacDougall
Jacket photograph ©Annie Griffiths Belt/
National Geographic/Getty Images
Map by Eric Leinberger
Printed and bound in Canada on ancient-forest-friendly paper by Friesens

Greystone Books gratefully acknowledges the Musqueam, Squamish,
and Tsleil-Waututh peoples on whose land our office is located.

Greystone Books thanks the Canada Council for the Arts,
the British Columbia Arts Council, the Province of British Columbia
through the Book Publishing Tax Credit, and the Government
of Canada for supporting our publishing activities.

Canada

{ CONTENTS }

Prelude · *viii*

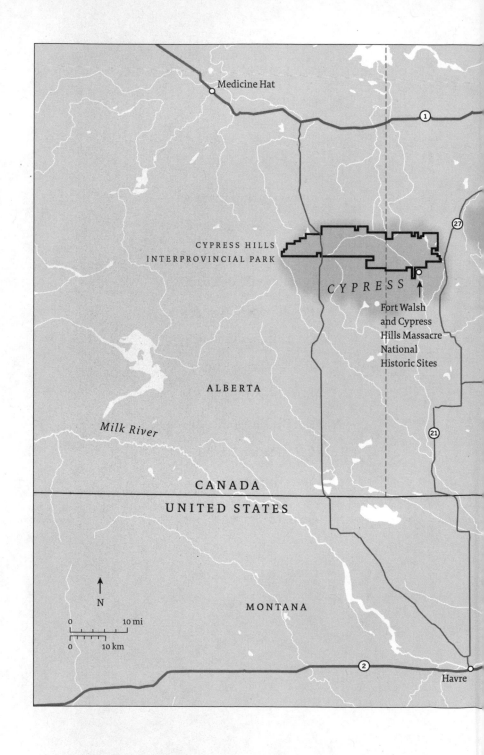

Medicine Hat

CYPRESS HILLS
INTERPROVINCIAL PARK

CYPRESS

Fort Walsh
and Cypress
Hills Massacre
National
Historic Sites

ALBERTA

Milk River

CANADA

UNITED STATES

N

0   10 mi

0   10 km

MONTANA

Havre

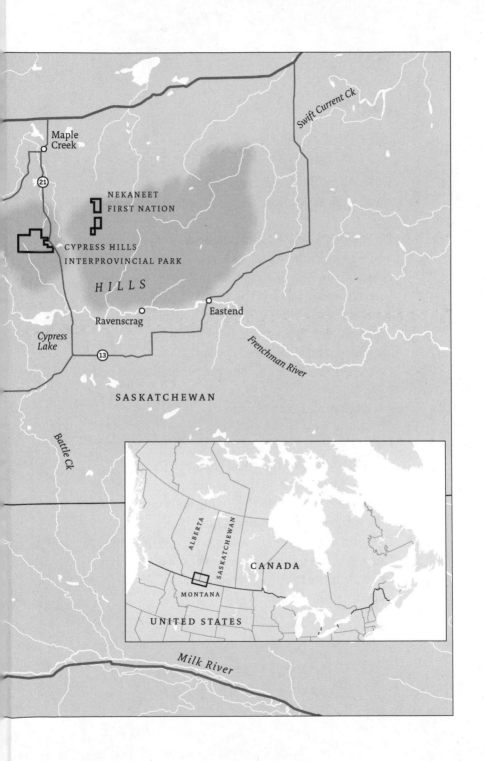

{PRELUDE}

We see them as a raven might see
them, from a distance.

The men walk single file, dark strokes etched
against an infinite plain of snow.
Behind them, a day's straggling march to the south,
lie a cold prison cell and the grim
accusing faces of the Great Father's blue-coated soldiers.
Ahead of them, if the spirits prove willing,
are friends and family, and the uncertain
embrace of the Great Mother and her red-coated police.

It is late November 1881, already
the dead of winter.

The men walk with the ghosts of the buffalo.
They are almost ghosts themselves.
The soldiers have taken their rifles and ammunition,
their torn lodges, their moccasins.
They are hungry. The snow stings their skin.
The police: it is hard to tell what the red coats
have taken, are taking. The truth.
Otapanihowin, the means of survival.

Black wings rasp against the frigid air.
Two men stumble, get up, fall.

The leader of the travelers, that Nekaneet
looks up, then looks ahead to the blue smudge
of hills on the horizon. *That means, just like
if we walk, if you are ahead, you are
kani'kanit, the leader.* Nekaneet is walking
north, walking home, walking into another day.
Somewhere up there in the distance,
you and I are waiting, hungry for stories.

ONE

GETTING THERE

...conceive a space that is filled with moving,
a space of time that is filled always filled with moving...
GERTRUDE STEIN, "The Gradual Making
of *The Making of Americans*," 1935

ET'S JUST say that it all began when Keith and I took a trip. Keith is Keith Bell, my companion of going on twenty years, and it's largely thanks to his love of travel that I've seen a bit of the world: the wild-and-woolly moors of Yorkshire, the plains of Tanzania, the barren reaches of Peninsula Valdés in Argentina. Yet the journey I want to tell you about was not a grand excursion to some exotic, faraway destination but a trip that brought us closer home. A nothing little ramble to nowheresville.

Remember what Thoreau once said about having "traveled a good deal in Concord," that insignificant market town in which he was born and mostly lived? In an unintended riff on this Thoreauvian concept, Keith and I find that we

have traveled a good deal in and around another insignificant dot on the map, a town called Eastend in our home
province of Saskatchewan.

Eastend, population six hundred, lies about a thumb's
breadth north of the Canada–U.S. border and more or less
equidistant from any place you're likely to have heard of
before. It's in the twilight zone where the plains of northern Montana meet and morph into the prairies of southern
Saskatchewan, a territory that leaves you fumbling with
highway maps. But if you piece the pages together, south
to north, east to west, and scribble a rough circle around
the centers of population—Great Falls, Calgary, Saskatoon,
Regina, Billings, and back to Great Falls again—you'll find
Eastend somewhere in the middle, a speck in the Big Empty
of the North American outback.

To explain how and why this out-of-the-way place has
become so central to our lives, I need to take you back several years, to a day in late September of 2000. Keith was just
embarking on a year-long sabbatical leave from his teaching
duties as an art historian at the University of Saskatchewan
in Saskatoon. As for me, I was supposed to be gathering
forces to meet the most daunting challenge of my writing
career. Earlier that summer, I had thrown common sense
to the winds and agreed to prepare a natural history of the
whole broad sweep of the western plains, from the Missis-
sippi to the Rockies and from the llanos of Texas north to
the wheat fields of Canada. By rights, I should have been at
my desk day and night, or in the crypts of the science library,
nose to the grindstone. What greater inducement could
there be for hitting the open road?

Happily for my guilty conscience, the route we had chosen for our travels that fall led directly into the heart of
my research. If I were going to write with authority about

grassland ecology (I told myself as I packed my holiday clothes), surely it was my duty to get up close and personal with my subject matter. I'm not entirely joking when I say that writing books is my way of getting an education.

And so off we set, Keith and I plus our three trusty canine companions—an aging retriever, a wire-haired dachshund, and a perky young schipperke—from our home in Saskatoon south under the big skies of Saskatchewan and Montana to our turnaround point, the tourist town of Cody in north-western Wyoming. From Cody, our return journey would take us north to Eastend, where we planned a brief layover before returning to our obligations in the city.

Cody, Wyoming, is an odd little town, and I am surprised to recollect that this trip marked the second time it had figured into our travel plans. On our earlier visit in the early 1990s, we had stayed in cheap digs along the highway, first at the Western 6 Gun Motel, where neon gunfire flared into the night from a sign at the entranceway, and then at the neighboring Three Bear Motel, where a trio of pathetic stuffed beasts, their mouths set in permanent snarls, stood guard over the check-in counter. This time around, several years older and more inclined to comfort, we'd gone upmarket to a respectable, if regrettably staid, establishment with a leafy courtyard.

Funny the things you remember, the things you forget. Even now, when so much else has faded from my mind, I could take you to the exact place we stayed in Cody, show you the room where we slept. See our boxy old blue van angled up to the building, its back doors swung open as we loaded it for the journey home. Hear our voices hanging in the thin morning air.

". . . binoculars?"

". . . water for the dogs? They say it's going to hit ninety."

"Any idea what we've done with the maps?" (Turns out that where I was headed could not be found on a map, though I had no way of knowing that at the outset.)

Although Cody's primary attraction for travelers is its proximity to Yellowstone National Park, an hour's drive to the west, the town prefers to see itself as a rootin' tootin' gateway to the past, to a West not merely of geography but of legend. From June to September, fake gunfighters confront each other in fake gunfights in the wide avenue outside the venerable Irma Hotel (Monday to Friday evenings at six and Saturday afternoons at two). Quite by accident, we'd caught them at it one evening, running around with their popguns and braying insults across the deserted street, under the guttering standard of the Stars and Stripes.

In this, as in so much else, the town takes its inspiration from its namesake and founding father, the late William Frederick Cody, better known as Buffalo Bill. As anyone who stops in town quickly becomes aware, Mr. B. Bill was an arresting character. A real-life participant in the conquest of the western plains, he had earned his spurs and his sobriquet in the 1860s when, as a scout for the U.S. Army and supplier to the Kansas Pacific Railway, he is said to have killed 4,860 buffalo in just eighteen months. That works out to about a dozen carcasses every twenty-four hours, assuming that he rested his trigger finger on the Sabbath.

Today, however, Buffalo Bill is remembered not so much for his actual exploits as for his pioneering success in transmuting those deeds into entertainment. In the spring of 1872, for example, Cody led Company B of the 3rd Cavalry in an attack against a camp of Mnikȟówožu, or Miniconjou, Lakota in Nebraska, an action for which he was immediately awarded a Congressional Medal of Honor. By December of that year, Cody had temporarily abandoned the field of battle to impersonate himself on stage, in a production entitled *The Scouts of the Prairies.* From that day forward, Buffalo Bill Cody seems to have inhabited a borderland between history and myth, between the gore and the glory of Western conquest.

Eventually, Cody's mastery of the facto-fictional mash-up would lead to his creation of Buffalo Bill's Wild West, a circus extravaganza in which real cowboys and real Indians engaged in mock skirmishes and a middle-aged easterner called Annie Oakley showcased the skills of a typical Western girl. This pioneering "reality show" earned Cody a place in the pantheon of American show business. But I have always been more impressed, or perhaps merely bewildered, by accounts of one of his lesser-known projects, a touring theatrical that hit the boards in the fall of 1876.

A few weeks earlier, General George Armstrong Custer had led the U.S. 7th Cavalry to a humiliating defeat at the hands of the Lakota, Northern Arapaho, and Northern Cheyenne near the Little Bighorn, or Greasy Grass, River (not far as the crow flies from Bill Cody's Wyoming headquarters). When word of this event reached him, he donned a black velvet costume adorned with silver buttons and lace that he wore in his stage shows and departed for the battlefield. There, he shot and scalped a Cheyenne chief named Yellow Hair, to avenge General Custer's "murder."

Back on the theatrical circuit, Cody was soon dramatizing this triumphant exploit in a production called *The Red Right Hand, or Buffalo Bill's First Scalp for Custer.* Although the evidence suggests that Yellow Hair was killed in a chance encounter, Cody presented the confrontation on stage as a face-to-face duel from which the better man had inevitably emerged as the victor.

On our first visit to town in the nineties, Keith and I had unexpectedly found ourselves staring at Yellow Hair's dishonored flesh. There it lay, parched and sallow, in a shiny glass case in the gracious halls of the Buffalo Bill Historical Center, still bearing the burden of Mr. Cody's triumphant slogan. "The first scalp for Custer," the museum tag read. This time, on our return visit, we had tiptoed through the galleries, almost afraid to look, but Yellow Hair's scalp had thankfully been removed from public contemplation.

LOOKING BACK, it seems fitting for our first journey to Eastend to begin under the aegis of Buffalo Bill. At the time, however, with no idea of what lies ahead, Keith and I are just a couple of happy, middle-aged kids getting our own show on the road. Life rests gently on our shoulders that morning as we load humans and dogs into our old van and point it in a northerly, homeward direction. Away we go, across the Shoshone River, around the shoulders of the Beartooth range, and then, joy to me, out and into the high red-rock moonscapes of northern Wyoming and south-central Montana. At the sporty resort village of Red Lodge, we turn our backs to the mountains and swing downslope into a landscape that's all space and sunlight and sky. My kind of country.

From Billings onward, we take the road less traveled, a narrow strip of asphalt that heads straight north through shimmering fields of stubble and herds of red-and-white cows. We stop for burgers at a town called Roundup, then sweep on through Grass Range without pause; side roads attempt to lure us off course to places named Fergus, Cat Creek, Heath.

The road and the country around it are so empty that every vehicle we meet demands comment. A red Silverado. Half an hour later, a black F-150. The drivers all boast big hats.

"I'm working on the wave," Keith says. "Do you use one finger or take your whole hand off the wheel?" Since I grew up in small prairie towns, as he didn't, he sometimes looks to me for advice about local etiquette. Even though he's lived in Saskatchewan for more than half his life—he arrived in Saskatoon in the mid-1970s—he still occasionally feels like a newcomer. No wonder, since he was born in Nairobi and educated there, at a boarding school in Scotland, and at universities in England. We had met in the fall of 1992 (only a year or two before our first trip to Cody, come to think of it) when he had found himself newly single and, in those days before online dating, had dared to place an ad in the personal column of the *Saskatoon Star-Phoenix:* "Friendly, attractive professional man, early 40s, seeks sincere, intelligent woman to enjoy adventures, travel, the arts . . ." I was then a youngish widow, with a freckle-faced daughter in tow: he had won me over at "friendly." We met, great jubilation ensued, and here we were together, going down the road.

About an hour past Grass Range, U.S. Route 191 flows down into the broad, sculpted valley of the Missouri River—we walk the dogs to the silvery, high-pitched clatter of the cottonwood leaves—and then we are up and away again, flying past the Little Rocky Mountains, the cusps of their blue molars biting into the western sky, past, almost without noticing, the Fort Belknap Indian Reservation, home to several hundred members of the Gros Ventre and Assiniboine nations. At the down-on-its-luck town of Malta, we turn west, through the not-much-luck-to-be-down-on hamlet of Chinook, and pass, again without noticing, a sign directing us to the Bear Paw battlefield, sixteen miles to the south. It was here, in the fall of 1877, that a massed force of U.S. infantry and cavalry, armed with a twelve-pound gun, surrounded, pounded, and eventually defeated a camp of Nez Perce refugees who, during the preceding months, had fought their way cross-country all the way from Oregon, in the desperate hope of finding safe haven on the other side of the international border.

At Havre, we jog north again, running for the border ourselves, and fail to notice, on the western outskirts of town, the remains of Fort Assinniboine, established in 1879 and once the grandest military establishment in Montana, with a garrison, at its peak, of more than five hundred blue-coated men. Their mission was to clear the country of "British" Indians, Cree and Métis hunters from across the line, by whatever means necessary. Voices hang in the air here, speaking of hunger, displacement, and cold, but we do not hear a word. Do you suppose it's really true that what you don't know can't hurt you?

FROM HAVRE onward, the land is reduced to a kind of primal simplicity, a tawny expanse that tugs our eyes to the farthermost edges of the world. Somewhere over there, in the white haze of distance, earth and heaven collide. Although I have always thought of myself as a prairie person, I am out of place here, dazzled by these spinning horizons and this unbounded sky that bleeds off into infinity. The prairie landscapes of my childhood had been softer, more contained. If instead of stopping at Eastend, Keith and I were to continue driving northwest clear across Alberta to the edge of the plains and into the scrubby fringes of the northern forest, and if we then pushed on through swamp spruce and muskeg for half a day more, we'd eventually break into the tree-fringed grasslands of the Grande Prairie in the Peace River Country. That's where I was born.

My parents were teachers, not farmers, so we always lived in town. But it was seldom far to the nearest pasture, where pale crocuses poked their furry snouts through the dead thatch first thing in spring and shooting stars launched their ardent magenta rockets around the margins of saline sloughs. As far as I knew, I was enjoying the total prairie package. But my mother knew differently. Her name was Edna Elizabeth Sherk, née Humphrey, and she was a true prairie girl, born to the high, wide, windswept plains of southern Alberta. She'd scarcely seen a tree in her life before coming north to the Peace River Country to teach, and at first they'd frightened her—so she told my sisters and me—looming over her in the darkness, rustling and shadowy.

She'd be in her glory here, I think, as I watch the light spin past the van. If it weren't for the occasional farm site with a struggling stand of box elders (or Manitoba maples, as they'd be called on the Canadian side of the line) braced against the wind, there wouldn't be a tree for fifty miles in any direction. At the international boundary, we pause momentarily for formalities, leaving behind the euphoric American promise of "Life, Liberty and the Pursuit of Happiness" for the less stirring Canadian virtues of "Peace, Order and Good Government." But the land flows on unmarked by national aspirations, as the road heads north and then east, on the final leg of our journey. By now, the day is fading, and we soon find ourselves tunneling through the dark. Highway signs leap into view, announcing places we have never heard of before: Consul, Robsart, Vidora. Even though we are theoretically back home, in our own country and province, the land that lies around us is enticing and unfamiliar.

We count down the miles to our destination, now so close at hand. There is nothing to be seen but liquid darkness, nothing to be heard but the gentle snoring of dogs and the hum of tires on asphalt. Then, with perhaps ten minutes to go, the headlights pick up a glimmer in the ditch, a flash of green-gold.

"Do you want to stop?"

Silly question. "Yes, of course!" We always stop.

In the wide bottom of the ditch, two coyotes are gnawing on the carcass of a road-killed deer. Caught in the flare of the headlights, their eyes glint; their muzzles are bloody; their bodies jitter in and out of the glare. There is something unexpectedly fleshy about them, something carnal and wild. We watch for a few minutes, then, with a nod of agreement, leave them to their feast. A door has opened into the darkness, giving us a privileged glimpse of the life that goes on, in secret, around us. A thrill of expectation rises in my body as we roll on toward Eastend. Whatever this place turns out to be, it's going to be an adventure.

EASTEND SITS on the southeastern edge of a landform known as the Cypress Hills. From the bit of reading I've done before leaving home, I know that "cypress" is a bungled translation, from Michif (the Métis language), of *les montagnes des cyprès*, a phrase that actually means Jackpine Mountains. In Blackfoot, these uplands have been known variously as the Eastern Place Where There Are Many Pines and as the Overlapping, or Wavelike, Hills. In Assiniboine, they're the place Where the Land Gets Broken; to some Cree speakers, the Beautiful Highlands. Like a great animal sprawled across the prairies, the hills rise in southeastern Alberta and flow eastward for more than eighty miles as a complex of broad, gradually diminishing plateaus. At the Head of the Mountain near Medicine Hat, the land stands almost 2,500 feet above the surrounding flatlands and attains a maximum altitude of nearly 5,000 feet, higher than the town of Banff—in fact, the highest elevation in Canada between the Rocky Mountain foothills and the mountains of Labrador. From this summit, a series of broken tablelands slouch downward across the Alberta-Saskatchewan border toward the Foot of the Mountain at Eastend. In all, the Cypress Hills encompass around a thousand square miles of magnificently varied terrain, a secret kingdom in the middle of a cactus plain.

Because of their abrupt rise above the surrounding prairie, the hill country experiences cooler temperatures and more precipitation than the dry lands at their base. Near the summit, conditions are ideal for conifers, including dark ranks of both jack and lodgepole pines, and for rare fescue grasslands. These isolated islands of habitat are occupied by isolated populations of birds and animals—white-throated sparrows, pine siskins, lynx, and elk—that are typically associated with the mountains and forests hundreds of miles to the west and north. At lower elevations, however, the boreal vegetation gives way to shining expanses of the ground-hugging grasses and wildflowers that are more typical of the northern plains. Wherever the land is broken, the hills have set a limit to the plow, and the wild prairie has been preserved as grazing land for cattle. As a result, the hills are an oasis of undisturbed prairie in a desert of plowed-up land and one of the most promising regions on the continent for grassland conservation.

Not surprisingly, the Cypress Hills are also celebrated across Saskatchewan as a beauty spot that everyone intends to visit, one day, soon, whenever they have a free weekend. But given the distance between this rise of land and the cities where most of us live, relatively few people actually make the trek. Before our arrival in Eastend, Keith knew the hills only as a vague presence on the horizon as he sped along the Trans-Canada toward Calgary and Banff. As for me, despite spending most of my adult life in the province (I, too, had arrived here from Alberta in the early 1970s), I had visited the area only twice before, never this far south, and never for more than two or three days at a time. But brief as those earlier visits had been, both had been riveting. Who could forget the slither of dozens of shiny garter snakes exploding out of their hillside hibernaculum on the first warm day in spring? Or, at the other end of a different year, the hard stare of a cow moose, with her calf at her side, warning off intruders at the bottom of a tobogganing slide?

Fortunately, Keith and I have booked a two-week stay in Eastend at the Wallace Stegner House: "First turn on your left when you get into town—there's a sign, so you can't miss it—and there'll be a key waiting for you in the front porch." I'd seen the place advertised in a writers' newsletter, so we knew that it was run by the Eastend Arts Council as a retreat where writers and other artists could pursue their creative interests. In the face of these lofty intentions, I blush to admit that what the place represented to us was two weeks of affordable accommodation. The only interests we intended to pursue were indolence and sloth, with the spice of excursions into the hills for excitement.

BY THE time we let ourselves into the house, all we could think of was sleep. Morning's light revealed a trim one-and-half-story structure with narrow gables, painted a soft sage green and screened from the street by a dense stand of spruce trees. Inside, past a cozy veranda furnished with armchairs and crocheted throws, lay a small but comfortable parlor, a dining room with a lovely old oak table, and a tidy kitchen stocked with a useful miscellany of dishes and gadgets. A narrow flight of wooden stairs led to a second floor that housed a bathroom, a drafty bedroom with a high metal-framed bed, and a scantily furnished space at the back that may have been intended as an office. I was relieved to discover that the table with which the room was equipped dated back to the pen-and-ink days and was too high, ergonomically speaking, for a writer with a laptop. Besides, there was no proper desk chair and no Internet service. Clearly, I could not be expected to do any serious work. Good, that was settled.

A bookcase outside the bedroom door offered an eclectic selection of reading material, including books by authors I recognized, from scanning the guest book downstairs, as previous visitors. And there were also several by the patron saint of the house, "the distinguished American writer" Wallace Stegner. I'd picked up that phrase from a plaque attached to an old water pump in the yard, which I'd had a chance to peruse when I'd gone out with the dogs. According to the engraved text, Stegner, then a small child, had lived in Eastend from 1914, the year the town was incorporated, until 1921. From 1917 onward, he and his family had lived in this very house, which had been designed and built by his father. The consummate local boy made good, Stegner had gone on to win both a National Book Award and the Pulitzer Prize for his fiction and had explored his Eastend experience in three of his works, *On a Darkling Plain, The Big Rock Candy Mountain,* and *Wolf Willow: A History, a Story, and a Memory of the Last Plains Frontier.*

I review this capsule biography in my mind as, one by one, I pull Stegner's books off the shelf. The only one I've heard of before is *Wolf Willow,* which I recognize as a memoir of his Saskatchewan boyhood. Over the years, people have occasionally told me that it's a book I "just have to read" and that I am "sure to love," but though I've tried it once or twice, I've never made much progress with it. Opening the book now at random, I come upon Stegner's description of the landscape that Keith and I have just been traveling through and that I have been struggling to fix into words.

"On that monotonous surface with its occasional ship-like farms, its atolls of shelter-belt trees, its level ring of horizon," Stegner writes, "there is little to interrupt the eye. Roads run straight between parallel lines of fence until they intersect the circle of the horizon. It is a landscape of circles, radii, perspective exercises—a country of geometry.

"Across its empty miles pours the pushing and shoulder-ing wind, a thing you tighten into as a trout tightens into fast water. It is a grassy, clean, exciting wind, with the smell of distance in it, and in its search for whatever it is look-ing for it turns over every wheat blade and head, every pale primrose, even the ground-hugging grass. It blows yellow-headed blackbirds and hawks and prairie sparrows around the air and ruffles the short tails of meadowlarks on fence posts. In collaboration with the light, it makes lovely and changeful what might otherwise be characterless."

In the past, I've sometimes wondered if what's kept me from reading *Wolf Willow* might be some subtle difference in national temperament between Yankee and Canuck, some slight shading of emotional dialect that does not translate precisely across the border. Apart from this shrine in East-end, it is remarkable how quickly Stegner's reputation and readership fade as you cross the line, reducing him in an instant from a lion of world literature to a regional writer and one-hit wonder. Who knows why?

But, now, face-to-face with Stegner's lyrical sentences, I am forced to concede that at least part of my resistance is easy to grasp. I am simply blindingly jealous! That trout shouldering into the wind. The wind that tosses us into the air with the birds, our senses reeling. I place the book care-fully back on the shelf, promising to return to it one day soon. For now, however, literature will have to wait: there are coyotes out there and deer and a world of wild things. It is time to load up our crew again and go exploring.

WITH THE benefit of hindsight, I can see that setting out on back roads in unfamiliar country, without detailed maps, through a landscape populated mainly by wildlife and half-wild cattle, and in a vehicle that was showing its age may not have been the smartest choice anyone ever made. And it didn't help that the weather, which had been unseasonably hot and summery all September, now blew in gray and mean. Undaunted—what did a little snow and rain mean to road warriors like us?—we decided for our maiden outing to head north and west on gravel roads, up and over the hills, to the town of Maple Creek, an hour or so distant. From there, after a bite of lunch, we would allow a paved highway to take us south and east, squaring the circle back to our starting point. Easy.

What we didn't know is that the back roads in the Cypress Hills are, to use the geologist's term, smectitic, a word that sounds like an expletive and that, in rough translation, means "turns to slime when wet." At first, everything went smoothly, as we pulled out of town on a well-graveled track and almost immediately found ourselves traveling through country so lovely it made my throat ache. On both sides of the road, the land swept away from the ditches as voluptuous as skin, and tidy barns and houses lay nestled into the cleavage of the hills. We stopped to watch as a flock of late-season bluebirds flashed against the dead grass, carrying the memory of summer on their backs.

It wasn't long, however, before our troubles began. As the road climbed gently toward the summit, conditions deteriorated apace, and soon we were viewing the scenery at odd angles, as we zigzagged from ditch to ditch. Somewhere along the way, a sign informed us, through thin drizzle, that we had attained the continental divide, whence waters flow south toward the Missouri River and the Gulf of Mexico and north to the South Saskatchewan River and the Arctic Ocean. This was an impressive kernel of information—who even knew that such a momentous height of land existed in flat old Saskatchewan?—and we would have paused to let its significance sink in if our van hadn't already been slithering, sideways and downward, in a northerly direction.

Eventually, hours later than intended and sprayed with mud from prow to stern, we made Maple Creek and the hard top, and all was forgiven. For as G.K. Chesterton once wisely pointed out, "An adventure is only an inconvenience rightly considered."[1] And so, the very next morning, we prepared to head out again. Prudently determined to stick to the pavement this time, our plan was to drive south and then east toward Grasslands National Park, the only public lands in Canada exclusively dedicated to prairie conserva- tion and our best hope to see burrowing owls, rattlesnakes, and the sole colony of prairie dogs north of the border. With good roads in prospect and a tail wind to help us on our way, surely everything would go perfectly. And so it did, for the first half hour or so. Then, in the middle of nowhere, with- out a bang or a sigh, our old van abruptly expired. No matter how often we turned the key or gazed longingly under the hood, nothing we did could persuade it to move an inch.

If you've never squeezed into the cab of a tow truck with three dogs, you really haven't lived. So there we were, envel- oped in clouds of warm dog breath, our vehicle dangling from a winch, forcibly returned to our starting point. Back in town, the mechanic at the gas station obligingly tweaked a thingamabob or two, replaced a widget that had blown, and expressed the hope that "she should be good to go." Thus reassured, we set out next morning for Fort Walsh, a historic post of the fabled North-West Mounted Police, which lies in a picturesque valley just west of Maple Creek. New destination, same story. Five minutes west of Eastend, the van sputtered to the side of the road, and there we were on the end of a winch, being dragged back home.

You might think that by now we'd have received the message, but not so. It was only after our fourth outing, and our third tow back to town, that we finally gave up and submitted to the inevitable. For the time being at least, we were going nowhere. On the surface, the cause of our predicament was obvious—some intractable mechanical problem, not surprising in our old tin can, perhaps brought on by unfriendly weather and lamentable road conditions. Crazy thing, though: that wasn't the way we felt. Instead of registering as an inconvenience, our dramatic returns to Eastend took on the aura of an intervention, as if some Power Greater Than Ourselves had resorted to the means at hand to grab hold of our attention. (Bad weather, maybe I could accept that, but did the gods really speak through clapped-out Astro vans?) It was ridiculous, we knew, but even though we laughed and shook our heads, we couldn't quite shake the sense that we were being offered a teaching moment. "Stop," a quiet voice kept saying. "Stay put. Pay attention to where you are."

In the week since we'd left Wyoming, Keith and I had been in ceaseless motion, traveling across boundaries, over watersheds, through memory and forgetting, knowledge and ignorance, in the uncharted territory between history and legend. Now we stood on the divide between the mundane and the numinous, between the events of our everyday lives and the meanings that were speaking to us. "Stay put," that still, small voice insisted. "Pay attention."

TWO

THE STEGNER HOUSE

Find yourself in the middle of nowhere.

FORMER EASTEND TOURISM SLOGAN

WHAT WE noticed first was the silence. If you stood on the curb in front of the Stegner House and listened, you could feel your ears reaching for sounds, as if they were trying to stand up as sharp as a coyote's. Now and then, a vehicle whispered along the main drag a couple of blocks to the south, and every hour or so a truck hauling a load of huge round bales growled down a gravel road on the western edge of town. But apart from these brief transgressions, the houses on both sides of the street seemed to lie in a trance, as if even the ticking of their clocks had been silenced.

In the kitchen of the Stegner House, the prevailing quiet was broken by an aged refrigerator, which wheezed asthmatically in the performance of its duties. When the wind blew, the storm windows rattled in sympathy and the rooms filled with the rhythmic, wavelike whooshing of the spruce trees in the front yard. But inexplicably these sounds served only to signal an eerie absence of noise. The black rotary telephone beside the dining-room table did not ring. Although our hosts had foreseen all of our basic needs and comforts, they had neglected to provide a radio, and the antiquated TV in the living room, equipped with rabbit ears, could emit little more than hiss. (Our attempts to watch the Canadians beat the U.S. 3–2 in the gold-medal game of the Women's World Hockey Championship came to naught because the action appeared to be taking place in a blizzard.) With the van consigned to dry dock for as-yet-undetermined repairs, we did not even have the benefit of the radio there. We had been cast adrift, with nothing to guide us but our thoughts and our unaided senses.

Morning after morning, Keith woke to report strange dreams, many of them about his father, who had died, in England, six months earlier. "I've never dreamed anything like that," he'd say, and then tell me how, in his sleep, he had looked at himself in a mirror and seen the face of his dead father looking back. Do you think it's this stillness? we asked each other. Do you think that staying busy, in constant commotion, is a way to keep from knowing what is really happening to us? Is that why people talk about "profound" silence? For my part, I slept dreamless, as if I were made out of wood, as if I were sleeping the rooted sleep of a poplar.

That was another thing: the dark. On clear, moonless nights just at bedtime, we'd often stand, shivering, in the backyard and gaze out into the universe. The darkness was as black as water, and you sensed that if you lost your footing, you might fall helpless into its depths. And the stars, stars beyond counting, streaming across the sky, all trillions of miles distant across an ether of space and time.

"Stay put," the voice had told us. "Pay attention to where you are." We were in the yard of the Stegner House, on Tamarack Street, in the town of Eastend, Saskatchewan, at the foot of the Cypress Hills. We were whirling through space on the skin of a living planet.

IN A town where everyone knows everyone else, visitors are painfully obvious. So we weren't surprised when, occasionally, someone stopped us on the street or in the grocery store and politely ran through the basics of who, what, why, when, and where. Were we enjoying our stay in Eastend? they'd ask in conclusion, and we were happy to oblige with a "yes." But the aisles of the Co-op, between the tea and the tinned beans, didn't really seem like the place to talk to strangers about our inner lives. Instead, I might say that it was a treat to see cottontails and white-tailed deer grazing on people's lawns. Or in a more expansive mood, I would rhapsodize about the view from the room at the top of the Stegner House (where I should have been working but wasn't, though they didn't need to know that) and the way the land drew your eyes from the backyard across the alley to the creek, with its fringe of willows, and then up and away to the hills. Strange, misshapen hills that made me think of ancient, fantastical worlds.

If the questioner seemed particularly sympathetic, I might even admit to the homely pleasures of nostalgia. For walking the streets of Eastend that autumn was like walking onto a set for the movie version of my childhood. Although the prairie towns of my youth were hundreds of miles distant and decades in the past, this place was almost as I remembered them. The grain elevators that presided over Railway Street, though strangely unbusy, recalled the dry, half-forgotten aromas of grain dust and "chop." The guys in ball caps who drew their half-tons up side by side in the middle of the main street looked familiar as they leaned out their cab windows to exchange shop talk. The kids on bicycles who, unafraid of strangers, stopped to talk to me and Keith could have been my childhood friends or models for paintings by Norman Rockwell. When the school bell rang to announce recess, it was all I could do to keep from hurrying over to the playground and looking for my own small self, shrieking with joyful dizziness on the merry-go-round or catching spiders in the tall grass along the fence.

If I were ever to lay claim to a hometown, it would have to be somewhere like this, a kind of simulacrum of all the places where my family had lived. Although my parents had both started out as teachers, my mother gave up her profession in the late 1940s to prepare for my birth, the first in what would become a family of three daughters. The result was that our family life, thereafter, was ruled by my father's career. Motivated sometimes by necessity and sometimes by boyish ambition, he moved from job to job and from success to success. Every time he changed jobs, and sometimes when he did not, we moved house. In my first fourteen years, we moved fourteen times.

I don't know how my mother put up with it, all that packing and unpacking, all that rending and rebuilding of life, but as a kid, I was remarkably open to the promise of a fresh start. Maybe this time I'd get a room of my own. Maybe the new town would have a better library than the last one or a befuddled, grandmotherly librarian who would pat me on the head and let me borrow books from the adult section. Yet even then, I sensed that these opportunities always came at a cost. With every move, we left behind friends and newly familiar places, losses that became more painful the more often they recurred. And even more troubling, because irrevocable, was the loss of a material connection to our personal past. Clothes we had outgrown, toys we no longer played with, doodles and scribblers stuffed into the bottom drawer of a desk: everything that we were unlikely to need in the future had to be discarded.

Why, I wondered, couldn't we be like the families I read about in books, who lived in mansions filled with treasures amassed in years long past by generations of swashbuckling uncles and shadowy spinster aunts? In particular, I yearned for an attic like the ones in which the young heroes and heroines of those novels launched their finest adventures, a midden of romantic old lamps, mysterious wardrobes, and battered trunks filled with lavender-scented letters.

"Did I ever tell you how I used to wish for an attic—" I ask Keith one day, but I can see that he's busy with his own thoughts. We are walking down the main drag in Eastend: on our right, we pass a romantic old brick bank that has been converted into a used bookstore. A few doors down, there's a mysterious storefront with a cracked window that, though vacant, still bears the boast of past glory as a "World Famous" antler exhibit. At the far end of the block, the former movie theater, somewhat battered but unbowed, carries the banner of the town's historical museum (at the moment unfortunately closed for the season).

"Look," Keith says, pointing up a side street toward a squat brown building shaded by cottonwoods. "Does that sign really say 'Cappuccino'?" Five minutes later, we are sipping espressos on the sunny patio at Alleykatz, an up-to-the-minute business that unexpectedly combines a coffee bar, a pottery studio, and a daycare. "Coffee, clay, and kids," as Deb, the proprietor, cheerfully informs us. Okay, so Eastend isn't just a collection of relics that have washed up from my past. It's a living, breathing town, a valiant little vessel that, though missing a mast here and a sheet there, is sailing against the trends of rural depopulation. (It must be the dazzle of the wind and sun on the poplar leaves that puts me in the mood for nautical imagery.) Keith and I linger on the deck for an hour or so, nursing our coffees, watching people come and go, and filling our lungs to the brim with contentment.

I HAD left small-town life for good, without the slightest twinge of regret, the year I finished high school; that was 1967. The quiet that I now found so consoling had been intolerable to me then, and I remember fuming about the airlessness of small-town thinking, the smug, white-gloves-on-Sunday assurance that there is one correct answer to each of life's questions. God was in His Heaven, all was right with the world, and history was progressing under His beneficent supervision. In school and in the pulpit, this comfortable self-assurance had frequently found expression in a homespun myth, the epic saga of Western settlement.

Here was a story so glorious that even my teenage cynicism could do little to tarnish it, a story in which I could cast myself, vicariously, among the heroines. Back in the 1700s, my own ancestors had left Europe, crossed a perilous ocean, and faced a wild continent rather than betray their heart's convictions. My dad's people had been Swiss Anabaptists who, in a quest for religious freedom, had fled first to Pennsylvania, then (as pacifist refugees from the American Revolution) to Upper Canada, and finally as pioneers to Alberta. My mom's family, though on the opposite side of the religious controversy, had followed a similarly convoluted path. They were Roman Catholics who, forced from

Portugal and then England, had settled in Maryland in the 1600s. When that refuge also failed them, they had resumed their migration, heading inland to settlements in Kentucky and then Missouri, before they too made the trek to the Canadian prairies.

Both lines had held strong to their religious convictions until the early 1900s, when at opposite ends of Alberta, my paternal grandfather and maternal grandmother had each broken with tradition by marrying outsiders. In other essentials, however, even these renegades remained true to the family heritage as they devoted their lives to bringing the prairie under cultivation and laying the groundwork of community life.

My parents had both grown up on homesteads, and my sisters and I used to beg our mother for stories of her childhood, as fabulous to us as Greek myths. Imagine riding to school on horseback or making butter with a stoneware churn or lying in the grass, watching fleets of flat-bottomed clouds float overhead. These borrowed memories came back to me here in Eastend, in the company of friendly ghosts, and especially during evenings in the Stegner House, itself a vestige of the pioneer era. Curled up on the couch in a pool of lamplight, with a dog at my feet, I again opened *Wolf Willow*, looking for confirmation of these honeyed stories.

What I found instead was an atmosphere of melancholy that I hadn't noticed in my earlier encounters with the book. "By most estimates," Stegner confessed in his opening chapter, "including most of the estimates of memory, Saskatchewan can be a pretty depressing country."[1] Despite his rapturous reappraisal of the landscape a few pages later—"grassy, clean, exciting"—his memories were permeated by a sour whiff of disappointment. Stegner's father had been a hard-luck gambler, a man who staked his family's future on 320 acres of sun-scorched, wind-scoured prairie a hard day's drive south of town and who then, through the consecutive misfortunes of wheat rust, fire, and drought, had lost the toss. "My father did not grow discouraged," Stegner recalled, "he grew furious. When he matched himself against something he wanted a chance to win. By 1920 he was already down in Montana scouting around for some new opportunity."[2] The family left for Great Falls the following year and then for Salt Lake City, where they settled in like a wind-blown drift of Russian thistles.

During their sojourn in Saskatchewan, the Stegners had spent summers on the homestead and winters in this house. It was here that, by Stegner's report, the entire family had nearly died in 1918 of the Spanish flu; here also that, in his words, "my grandmother 'went crazy' and had to be taken away by a Mountie to the Provincial asylum because she took to standing silently in the door of the room where my brother and I slept—just hovered there for heaven knows how long before someone discovered her watching and listening in the dark."[3] In the cozy kitchen a few paces from where I sat reading, Stegner's father had once "clouted [him] with a chunk of stove wood," sent him flying across the room, and broken his collarbone. The shadows cast by the lamp seemed to deepen, and the silence gathered as I read; these traumas were too close for comfort.

Fortunately for my peace of mind, the members of the Eastend Arts Council had provided another account of the settler experience that struck a more cheerful note. A weighty volume, bound in green and emblazoned with gold, too large for the bookshelves upstairs, it was tucked away with the phone book on the telephone table. Entitled *Range*

Riders and Sodbusters, it had been published by the local historical society in 1984 as a tribute to "our" pioneers. "We
record these stories with awe," the editors wrote, aware
"that this area had its definite beginnings in these stories
never again to be relived and an era in history never to be
repeated."[4]

Completely typical of the genre—books like this one had
been compiled in communities across the prairies as the
old-timers began to fade, including a couple that featured
members of my own family—it consisted of capsule biog-
raphies of the founding fathers and, somewhat grudgingly,
the founding mothers of the area. Who could resist the smil-
ing faces that gazed shyly out of these pages or their stories
of heroic determination?

One of the pictures that caught my eye showed an
atypically somber-faced man in a three-piece suit, standing aslant to the camera and clasping the hand of a sturdy
woman with back-swept hair and a foursquare stance.
Their names were Edmond and Marie Nibus. As Marie proceeds to explain, they had come to Canada from Belgium
in 1912, along with their five-year-old son, and arrived on
their homestead, in the middle of a blizzard, the following
autumn. Their first home on the prairie was a two-room
shack, punctured with knot holes and furnished with little
more than a stove, a table, and a bunch of apple boxes. "It had
a brand new board floor," Marie recalled, "and I thought it
was wonderful."

"Life on a homestead had a lot of hardships," she continued. "I think young ones are spoiled nowadays. Many were
the days that I'd go out and disc with four horses. I had
to take [son] Leon with me and he sat on my knees while I
drove. We'd stay out from morning till evening, then figured

that the horses needed a rest." [5] (Ed, meanwhile, was working for neighbors to earn some much-needed cash.) A note
at the end of the entry informs us that Marie and Ed lived
and worked on their farm until 1954, when they retired into
town. They died there, aged 94 and 101 respectively, in the
early 1970s, shortly after celebrating their sixty-fourth wed-
ding anniversary.

I spent hours leafing through the volume, with its
tales of runaway horses and broken machinery, lightning
strikes and blizzards, good crops and bad, all animated by
a surprising lightness of spirit. Even the 1918 influenza
epidemic, which had taken the lives of so many and left a
bruise on Wallace Stegner's thoughts, could be construed
as having unexpected benefits. "There was an atmosphere
of 'togetherness'... that united the community," one survivor recalled. "Truly these folks were the best in the world." [6]
Reading between the lines, it appeared that this same
togetherness had helped to bring the community through
the terrible thirties drought. "With no crops, no money, in
debt and on relief, times were hard," one old-timer admitted,
"but we got along somehow... There were picnics, dances
and parties. The women would bring lunch and the men
paid a quarter. Part of this bought the coffee, and the fid-
dlers were given the rest." [7]

Hard work and fiddle tunes, bread and roses. Through
sheer stick-to-it-iveness, these dauntless people had created not only farms and ranches but also churches, libraries,
hospitals, and schools. They had played in dance bands,
organized Christmas concerts, and planned community
fairs; they had raised flocks of children and grandchildren
and great-grandchildren. Even though I had never met any
of these people, I recognized them as my own. Here I was in
Eastend, home away from home.

ONE MORNING, Keith and I decided to treat ourselves to breakfast at Eastend's premiere dining establishment. Jack's Café is on the main drag, a couple of doors up from the late-and-lamented antler museum. Very much a going concern, it is nonetheless also a blast from the past, complete with a soda fountain, a glass cabinet full of pies, and, on the wall, one of those old-fashioned rotary displays that flips from ad to ad. Fabrics and Notions, flip. Livestock Hauling, flip. Septic Service, flip. One of the oldest surviving businesses in town (a tidbit I had picked up from the local history book), it had been founded by immigrants from the Peloponnese, of all places, around 1920 and then lovingly passed down, from hand to hand, to a succession of Greek-Canadians. One husband-and-wife team, George and Angela Doolias, had become so renowned for their steaks and Greek specialties that they earned annual listings in *Where to Eat in Canada*, the national guide to fine dining.

When you order pancakes at Jack's, you get pancakes: they arrived three high and large as platters, with sausages on the side and cups of acrid coffee to wash them down. As Keith and I attempted to do justice to this munificence, we had plenty of time to look around and admire our surroundings. It wasn't just the vintage fittings that caught our attention, as charming as they were. Angie Doolias was not just a restaurateur; she was also an artist. From counter height to ceiling, all around the room—jogging above the cabinets, slipping over doors, flowing seamlessly around corners—the room was encircled by a mural.

Beginning on the north wall, above the cash register and partially obscured by a Coke machine, it showed the primordial prairie landscape, unpeopled and untouched, grazed by herds of buffalo and overflown by a golden eagle. Moving around to the east, humans enter the scene, and we see them driving buffalo over a cliff and, later, pitching their tipis in a broad valley. But change is coming, just around the bend. Beyond the pies and above the door to the kitchen, a column of covered wagons is wending its way toward a fort, led by a pair of riders in red-serge tunics and pillbox caps. Clearly, these are not the blue-coated fighting men that so stirred Bill Cody's pride. Instead, as a loyal Canadian, Doolias has memorialized the arrival of the North-West Mounted Police at what I assume must be Fort Walsh. With law and order now assured, the pageant of progress picks up, as home-steaders break the sod with oxen along the south wall and a train steams into the station of a nascent Eastend in the southwest corner. If you look closely, you can see Jack's Café already in place, between the bank and the hotel.

I'm guessing that it was at about this point in the cre-ation of the mural when two Aboriginal men came into Jack's for lunch. (I have this story from a friend who hap-pened to be there at the right moment.) "Where's it going to end?" one of the diners asked the artist, as he surveyed what she had done. "With a mushroom cloud?"

"No," George Doolias shot back, coming to his wife's aid. "It'll be two Native guys in a Lincoln, pit-lamping deer." Everyone had a good laugh.

But of course the mural does not end with a nuclear apoc-alypse or with poachers, either. In fact, Aboriginal people have disappeared from the action halfway around the room, as if they have no part to play, for good or ill, after the incom-ers appear. Instead, as the mural rounds the home stretch onto its final wall, it celebrates the fulfillment of the settlers' dream, with a century of technological advancement and plenty. The story draws to its triumphant conclusion above a bank of orange plush booths in the northwest corner of the café. In the foreground a pair of combines plies the fields of a prosperous, modern farm, its yard lined with shiny bins poised to receive the golden harvest. In the middle distance, a landscape once dotted with buffalo is now studded with oil wells, and the crenellated skyline of Calgary lures the eye, ever onward, into the future.

THAT EVENING, I stood in the yard of the Stegner House, under a sky quilted with clouds, and listened to the yip-yip-yipping of coyotes on the hills above town. Tell the truth. Although I had been brought up on the Creation Story of prairie settlement and, as the past few days had proven, was still susceptible to its charms, I was no longer a true believer. It was one thing to sit in Jack's Café, blissed out on maple syrup, and enjoy a confident portrayal of the pageant of progress. But did I really believe that a prairie landscape dominated by pump jacks and industrial agriculture is, in any ultimate sense, an improvement on the now-shattered buffalo eco-system? And while it had been entertaining and, yes, even inspiring, to sit with the local history and recall my debt to the people who had planted me here, did I really believe that the West had been won while whistling a happy tune?

If I interrogated my memory, I could hear my mother's voice turn brittle when she spoke, as she rarely did, of the beatings her own father had inflicted on his sons, but not his daughters, violent explosions of rage that seemed out of proportion to youthful misdeeds. Frustration refracted into cruelty. The Stegners, with their two sons, had been able to pull up stakes and leave when things turned sour on them; the Humphreys, with a brood of ten, did not have that option. They had toughed it out on a bankrupt farm, too proud to accept relief—but not too proud, in my mother's nightmare recollection, to attempt to abandon a promising little girl, her own small self, to the care of a more prosperous neighbor. When she told me this story eighty years later, her voice still cracked with grief. Perhaps I had been avoiding *Wolf Willow* out of mere cowardice, a reluctance to face home truths when they were offered.

The night wind had an icy bite and it chased me back indoors, past Keith dozing on the couch and up the narrow stairway to the back room, where young Wally and his brother had once slept. With the spectre of their bewildered grandmother in the hallway behind me, I gazed out the window into the heavy dark and recalled how my own sense of Western history had, over the years, gradually come unmoored. I remembered sitting in Sunday school one morning (in the minister's study at First United Church in Vermilion, Alberta, to be precise) and suddenly seeing with irrevocable clarity that the assurances of Christianity, and of a divinely ordained plan, were an illusion. This revelation left me with little to show for my religious upbringing except the Golden Rule and a slightly idiosyncratic version of a favorite children's hymn:

> All things bright and beautiful
> All creatures great and small
> All things *wild* and wonderful . . .

I thought of the day, a few years later, when I looked down on the prairie from an airplane and for the first time saw how the curvilinear contours of hill and valley, with their scribbled water courses, seemed to struggle against the straight lines of the surveyors' rule. This wild and wonderful land was caught tight in a net, and my people, and others like them, had ensnared it.

And there was something else. On the homestead in the Peace River Country where my dad grew up, there was, and is, a piece of land known affectionately within the family as the Indian Quarter. Closer to a half-section in reality, it consists of a cultivated field bisected by a track that leads to a brushy ridge. Past this horizon, the land folds downward, through a tangle of aspen and spruce, to the wild currents of the Beaverlodge River. On the grassy ledge beside the water, the whole family often gathered together when I was a kid—a happy tribe of aunts, uncles, and cousins—to picnic and swim in summer or, when the ice was clear, to skate and drink hot chocolate on winter afternoons.

According to the family story, this spot had once been a favorite stopping place of the local Beaver Indians, who had continued to camp here until about 1910, when my pioneering great-grandfather and his sons had purchased the property from them. Like many family legends, this account is at least partly false, since treaty Indians at that time were not permitted to hold individual title to land. But whatever the truth of the matter, I was fascinated by the thought of those disappeared encampments and of the people who had lived in them. Now we were here, enjoying ourselves, and they had vanished.

I'm not sure how old I was when this discomfort first coalesced into an image, though I may have been eight or nine. In my mind's eye, I saw my late grandmother (think Queen Victoria in a housedress) crossing the field on the dirt track that led toward the riverbank. Opposite her, at a distance, a young Beaver woman (an Indian princess in buckskin) stood at the edge of the brush, as if she had just come up the hill from the water. The two women faced each other across the clearing, as diffident as stones. No matter how often I conjured them there, they never approached each other, and neither uttered a word. The silence that lay between them seemed impenetrable.

NIGHTS PASSED, and days, and our two-week booking at the Stegner House was drawing to a close. Our van turned up, roadworthy, with a little time to spare, but to our surprise we no longer wanted to go anywhere. Keith had settled into a happy routine of reading in the backyard—summer having graced us with a brief return—or just sitting and looking across the creek at the sun-cured hills. The land was tawny, streaked with black in the gullies where brush flowed down the slopes, and it reminded him, in a distant way, of his East African boyhood.

Stay put, the quiet voice had told us. Pay attention to where you are. We were in Eastend, Saskatchewan, on the northernmost edge of the great North American plains. We were traveling through time, through memory, the invisible dimension.

And then, before we quite knew what had happened, our holiday had sped past, and we were back in the city, bound to our desks. Although we often spoke of our time in Eastend—I mean, really, a cappuccino bar in a beat-up prairie town, and coyotes singing in the dark, and the light spinning around the cottonwoods, and the lure of all those places we had tried to get to and hadn't, and the unheralded sense of euphoria that had overtaken us by the time we left—despite all that, not to mention our unexpected immersion in the settlement saga and the connections with our own pasts, we had no expectation that we'd be coming back.

Yet when we hit the road the following summer on another of my grassland research tours, guess where we ended up? It seemed that all roads led to Eastend. When we noticed a tidy white bungalow for sale on Tamarack Street, a block north of the Stegner House—and when we bought it—we knew that we were hooked. This homely little town in its nest of wild hills had charmed us into putting down tentative roots. And all around, the bright wind whispered through the grass, speaking to us of reasons we didn't yet understand.

[THREE]

DIGGING IN

This was, after all, the kind of landscape
that demanded one's attention.

BETH LADOW, *The Medicine Line*, 2001

B Y THE time the house deal had gone through, it was September, and another prairie winter was drawing near.
You could hear it in the metallic rattle of the cottonwoods across the alley from our new house; you could see it
in the fiery red of the chokecherry bushes along the creek.

Our new house. All that fall and winter, whenever we had
a free weekend, we filled our van to the gunnels with household paraphernalia, loaded up the dogs and headed for what
had suddenly become our second home. In choosing a route
for our travels, we were as unvarying as pilgrims. After an
hour or so in the fast lane on the highway to Calgary, we left
the mainstream at Rosetown to head south into a big silent
country under a high blue sky. Merely to think about it now,
sitting at my desk, makes my chest expand with breath, as if
the only response to that light and space were to open into it.

From that moment on, the journey became easy, and we seemed to flow effortlessly downhill, first heading south to cross the impounded waters of the South Saskatchewan River, a liquid plain set among tawny slopes, and then on to the leafy valley city of Swift Current. From there it was west to Gull Lake, south to Shaunavon, and finally west again, proceeding step by diminishing step toward our destination.

From the beginning to the end of the journey—a good four hours of travel, with a few minutes added here and there as rest stops for humans and dogs—the landscape told and retold the same familiar story. The broad fields of stubble that spun by our windows represented the climax of the settlement saga, the triumphant end point of the mural in Jack's Café, the payday of my own grandparents' enterprise. Somewhere past Gull Lake, we passed a commemoration of the whole agricultural undertaking, painted in exact letters on the gable of a meticulously maintained barn: "Rolling View Farm," it read, "1917." It was as if the settlement experience marked the beginning of time.

Of the country's longer past and its deep reservoirs of stories—memories of the Métis settlement that (unbeknownst to me on these early journeys) flourished briefly at the Saskatchewan River crossing; of the terrible battle that had taken place in the Red Ochre Hills, southwest of Swift Current, in 1866; or of the buffalo jump near Gull Lake that dates back thousands of years and once sustained hundreds of families—of these memories and so many others we did not hear a single word.

By the time we reached Shaunavon and the last, short, westward leg of our journey, the countryside had become assertively modern, with pump jacks feeding in the stubble like dazed, mechanical birds. Yet in the face of this evidence of "progress"—and who was I to knock it, whizzing along as I was in a gasoline-powered van?—I found my eyes wandering around and past these intrusions to consider the lay of the land. On the western horizon up ahead, the world was now rimmed by a blue rise of hills, which suggested that our destination was drawing close. Meanwhile, to the north of the road and to the south and then, at irregular intervals, here and there, near and farther afield, we found ourselves surrounded by a flotilla of strange landforms.

"Look," I said to Keith, beside me in the driver's seat, "those hills—they're like whales, bigger than whales, stranded under the grass."

"Eskers, drumlins, and kames," he replied smartly. (He was an art historian: how did he know this stuff?) "That's all I remember from A-level geography. Something to do with glaciers and the Ice Age." Drumlins. That was it: I'd just been reading about them, as part of the research for the chapter on geological history in my prairie book.

"Hey," I said, "I know about this. The geologists call it a swarm. We're driving through a ten-thousand-year-old drumlin swarm."

A year earlier, approaching Eastend from the south, we'd been ushered into town by coyotes, distorted forms caught in the headlights' glare. Now, arriving from an approximately opposite direction, we found ourselves in the company of a troupe of Ice Age hills, their ancient energy held in suspended animation. And more strangeness was in store as we rounded the final bend and rolled down into the wide bottomlands of the Frenchman River valley. Instead of proceeding into town as we had expected, we appeared to be heading straight for an earthwork of ridges and conical, turretlike hills that blocked the view ahead. At the very last minute, the road jogged left, discovered a gap, and delivered us into town and onto the main drag. A sign announced that we had entered the Valley of Hidden Secrets.

OUR NEW house was essentially perfect as found. Built in the early 1970s, it featured mahogany-fronted cabinets, complete with copper-trimmed knobs, and a planter-knick-knack-and-book-shelf combo that was straight out of my teenage years. Even the crimson carpet in the bedroom— "This will need to be updated," the real-estate agent who showed us the place had told us solemnly—exuded a shabby, retro charm. The real glory of the place, however, was not its stylish accoutrements but what in a more competitive market might have been written up as its "prime location, surrounded by parks."

Our place was at the very end of the street, on the outer-most edge of town. Beyond the back fence, across the alley, lay the bend of the Frenchman River where young Wallace Stegner and his friends had once congregated to swim. To the north lay a wide grassy field, really a floodplain, that was bounded by a sweeping arc of the stream and housed the town's baseball diamonds and campground. Past these amenities and across the creek, the land rose up and away from us in a choppy sea of conical mounds, intercut by coulees and shadowed by a tangle of chokecherries and rosebushes. The wide prairie world was right there, on the other side of the wall, just begging for us to come out and continue our explorations.

Strangely, however, the house turned a blind eye to this view. Although there were openings in every other direction, east, west, and south, the entire north wall was windowless. We were loftily critical of what we saw as an aesthetic error, until someone pointed out that the previous owners might not have looked at the scene through quite the same lens as us. The Taylors—we knew their name from a decorative knocker affixed to the front·door—had been ranchers who spent summers somewhere up in the hills and retreated to this house in the fall, much as the Stegners had done a generation before. (All this we gleaned from conversations with our new neighbors.) Perhaps, like coastal fishing families who face their homes away from the sea, the Taylors had preferred to turn their backs on the prairie and its lethal winter storms. Keith and I, by contrast, were mere visitors, in the country though not yet of it. Regardless of wind and weather, the prairie was calling to us and we were eager to open ourselves to its wide horizons.

In remarkably short order, we had cajoled a local contractor into ordering a picture window (four-paned to echo the four-paned knickknack shelves in the room divider) and inserting it into our living room wall. Now, with our brand new secondhand love seat positioned directly in front of the glass, we could sit side by side and gaze out at the scene: from the bare symmetry of the poplar tree in the foreground to the dense scrawl of bushes along the river and then up, layer by layer, fold upon voluptuous fold, to the bony haunches of the hills that loomed over the town. Sometimes, we watched as small herds of white-tailed deer grazed on the flats along the stream bank or held our breath as they circled close, doe eyed and fleshy, and walked under our windowsill. Above them, against a leaden sky, the snowy hills told the hours in shadowed pools of blue that spread and deepened and finally merged into the darkness.

AND THEN it was spring, and life settled into a pattern that has served us well ever since. Although we spend most of our time in the city, we make a point of getting to Eastend at least once a month. During the university term, when Keith is occupied with lectures and meetings, we usually only manage three or four days at a time, but in summer, when the pressure is off, we often have the luxury of settling in for a span of weeks. Over the years, the balky old van to which we owe our Eastend adventure has given way to more reliable wheels, and the dogs who accompanied us on our early travels have all died and been replaced, sometimes in super-abundance. These days we are accompanied by two retrievers in the back seat and two dachshunds up front, with Calla the cat wedged in somewhere or other. In recent years, for longer stays we have rounded out the menagerie with two quarter horse geldings, Tanner and Tex, whom we tug along behind us in a horse trailer.

By the time we have reached our destination, delivered the horses to their rented pasture (an idyllic valley with a spring-fed creek), and settled in, Keith and I are usually content to sit and stare out our new window for an hour or two. But before long, the view, plus a barrage of canine entreaties, lures us out the door. Sometimes, we stroll down the back alley and across a narrow margin of grass to stand on the cutbank and gaze down into the slow, syrupy water of the Frenchman River. As a student of *Wolf Willow*, I know that Wallace Stegner stood on this very spot when he visited town on a reconnaissance mission in the early 1960s (shyly, slyly, giving his name as Mr. Page), impelled by "the queer adult compulsion to return to one's beginnings." [1] And it was here, electrified by the "tantalizing and ambiguous and wholly native" musk of the wolf willow, that he reconnected with the "sensuous little savage" he had once been. [2]

For newcomers like us, however, the excitement is more immediate. Look, see that sudden shimmer down there in the water, by the old piling? It's a beaver, a muskrat; no, it's a mink, swimming upstream, impossibly black and shiny. Or follow the river back toward our house and west around the first bend, no more than a hundred steps, and stop on the bank again. Do you hear a catbird mewing in the bushes; notice the kingbirds hawking for insects from the low, overhanging branches; see the swallows, lithe as fish, slicing through the air? Try to follow their acrobatics with your binoculars and all you'll get is blur. Barn swallows, check. Bank swallows, check. Tree swallows, check. Northern roughwinged swallows, check. Violet-green swallows, check. Who would ever have guessed that they could be so swift, so blue, so varied, so alive? So thrilling.

"Biodiversity" is a bloodless term but here it was, on the wing. The wild tangle of life along the creek bank offered a moment of grace, exempt from decline and loss, in which beauty coexisted with abundance. As a student of grassland ecology, I knew that this was a rare and privileged experience, a dispensation from the ecological tragedy of the Great Plains grasslands. Back in the city, my office was strewn with reports that attempted to quantify everything that had been lost: number of acres given over to cultivation, percentage of wetlands drained, the extent to which prairie rivers have been channelized or curtailed. Other documents tallied the body counts of the disappeared and the dead—plains grizzlies, plains wolves, pronghorns, prairie dogs, prairie chickens, sage grouse—all the special creatures of the grasslands that are either long gone or grievously diminished in numbers.

Leading the list is the plains buffalo, known with scientific insistence as *Bison bison bison,* an animal whose hair was once woven into every bird's nest, whose hooves aerated the tough prairie sod, and whose flesh fed tribes of hunters, both two- and four-legged. Massed into herds of hundreds and thousands, the buffalo flowed across the landscape, eating on the run, and creating a textured mosaic of grazed and ungrazed habitats. Diverse habitats for the prairie's diverse organisms. Even the buffalo's dung played a role by helping to sustain the invisible universe of the soil.

The special genius of the grassland ecosystem is its ability to ride the extremes of a midcontinental climate— a meteorological rollercoaster of blazing heat, brutal cold, sudden downpours, and decades-long droughts—by storing precious moisture and nutrients in the ground. As much as ninety percent of the biological activity in the grasslands takes place in the soil. When this life force puts up shoots, the vegetation may look meager and stunted, but it is bursting with energy. The power of the soil, the wind, and the rain is concentrated in every leathery shrub and every blade of sun-cured grass. Transferred up the food chain, this vitality takes on animal form and becomes manifest in the blue of a butterfly, the bright eye of a snake, the eerie voice of a curlew echoing over a lonely landscape.

But the truest expression of the grasslands, without any doubt, was the buffalo. What would it have been like to put your ear to the ground and feel the rumbling vibration of thousands of hooves running across the plains, somewhere out of sight? What if we could step back a lifetime or two, to 1873, and ride south from the Cypress Hills, day after day for a week, with buffalo on all sides?

> The great herd running away,
> The buffalo running,
> Their drumming hooves
> Send dust clouds billowing to the sky
> And promise good hunting
> The buffalo and her child approaching,

Mother and Calf coming
Turned back from the herd,
Promise abundance.[3]

Once the heart and soul of the prairie ecosystem, the
buffalo is now described by scientists with the International
Union for Conservation of Nature as "ecologically extinct."
Although today's herds number in the tens of thousands,
virtually all of the survivors endure a hemmed-in, semi-
domesticated existence as commercial livestock and park
specimens.

Worse yet is the news that damage to prairie ecosys-
tems is not limited to the past. Even now, the populations
of grassland birds—from chestnut-collared longspurs to
Sprague's pipits and from bobolinks to burrowing owls—are
decreasing year by year, exhibiting faster and more con-
sistent declines than any other similar habitat group. The
latest data indicate that aerial insectivores, including the
nighthawks that dart over Eastend on summer evenings and
the swallows that dance along the creek, are also experienc-
ing a calamity. Nobody knows why the populations of these
species have dropped so sharply, but the general consensus
is that the remaining grasslands are so impoverished that
they can no longer provide the birds with what they need to
survive in abundance.

And yet here in the Frenchman Valley, the mink are still
side-slipping into the moist grasses at the edge of the water
the way they have always done, and the rough-winged swallows nest in cutbanks along the river just as they did when
Wallace Stegner was young. Despite everything that has
been lost and everything we are now losing, the landscape
around Eastend remains radiant with life. Imagine walking down the main drag at dusk and looking up to the beat

of powerful white wings, as a flight of swans whooshes low overhead, following the course of the street. Imagine the hollow *hoo-hoo-hooing* of great horned owls in the trees outside your house. Breathe in and fill your lungs with reassurance. Breathe out and exhale your grief. Give yourself permission to walk in beauty.

THE BUFFALO ecosystem—the wild prairie—is irreclaimably lost and gone, but its spirit continues to linger in the hills and valleys around Eastend. If my initial experience of the town had brought on a bout of childhood nostalgia, our encounters with the life along the creekside invoked a deeper, earthier past. And Eastend had another source of consolation to offer, though I didn't recognize it as such at first. After all, you don't typically expect to find comfort in a dinosaur museum. The T.rex Discovery Centre is Eastend's marquee attraction, and like everything else in town, it is an easy few minutes' walk from our house. To get there, you simply walk out the back door and down the alley (past the old swimming hole and Stegner's childhood home), take a sharp turn to the right, and cross the river on an old iron bridge. At a T-junction, a yellow-and-black traffic sign may urge you to continue up the north hill, with a promise or perhaps a threat. It reads: *T.rex Dead Ahead.*

And there's our goal, set into the hillside and fronted by a sleek curtain of silvery glass. Officially opened in 2003 as a joint project of this jaunty little community and the Royal Saskatchewan Museum, the center houses the fossilized remains of "Scotty," one of the most complete tyrannosaurus skeletons ever uncovered. Most of her bones (for, yes, Scotty turned out to be *regina* rather than *rex*) are stored, together with thousands of other wonders, in the state-of-the-art paleontology laboratory that's to your right as you enter the wide front doors. Even so, her terrible presence dominates the place. She bears down on you from the life-sized mural in the main display gallery, gape jawed and toothy. She leers from a nearby plinth, a disembodied head with cold snake eyes and scaly skin. If I were the triceratops displayed on a nearby bench, I'd seriously consider making a run for it.

Scotty was a Late Cretaceous predator that lived, and died, about sixty-five million years ago. Thereafter (until 1991, when a worn tooth and caudal vertebra were found protruding from the dirt) her mineralized bones lay entombed in a bleak, arid tributary of the Frenchman River, about half an hour's drive southeast of town. Officially known as Chambery Coulee, the quarry is fondly regarded by paleontologists as "the Supermarket of the Dinosaurs." In and around Scotty's disarticulated bones lie the traces of an entire extinct world: fish scales, turtle skulls, champsosaur ribs, crocodile teeth, the frail tibiotarsus of a long-dead bird. Here, too, are the fragmented remains of *Edmontonsaurus saskatchewanensis* (the typical duck-billed dinosaur of the Late Cretaceous era) and of *Triceratops horridus* (sometimes crushed within fossilized T. rex dung). The triangular tooth of a pachycephalosaurus, the fang of a dromaeosaurid, or raptor.

It takes a few rounds of the gallery to begin to take everything in. These monstrous, fantastical beasts, with their horns and their fins and their bird-feet, had lived in a lush subtropical forest near the shore of an inland sea. They had lived and been buried *here*. And to think that I had been getting all tingly when I picked up echoes from my childhood or, across mere centuries, conjured up the vanished abundance of the buffalo prairie. Now I was being invited to stride lightly back over millions of years, to confront the final days of the Age of Reptiles. Relatively soon after Scotty died, a massive asteroid crashed into the Gulf of Mexico (near the present-day town of Chicxulub) with the force of a hundred million megatons of TNT, causing an apocalypse of tsunamis, earthquakes, volcanic eruptions, incandescent ejecta, and a pall of ash and dust that enveloped the planet. This cataclysm marked the end of the terrible lizards.

And yet, out of this cosmic disaster, strange new life was born. Could it be that the mad genius of evolution is more ruthless and resourceful than we give it credit for? Perhaps, despite all of humanity's worst efforts and the extinction crisis that we are bringing down on our own heads, life will eventually flood the world with its new inventions, as beautiful and grotesque as those that have been lost to the ravages of the past. It's a brutal hope, but hope nonetheless.

At the T.rex Centre, crossing the threshold of mass extinction is as simple as stepping through a door. Leaving Scotty and Co. behind, we proceed through an archway and find ourselves circling around the spotlit skeleton of yet another gargantuan beast, this one sporting humped shoulders; a scooped-out, square-jawed skull; and a pair of bony spurs that sprout from what must have been its snout. A caption identifies it as a brontothere, or "thunder beast," a long-vanished relative of the rhinoceros and the horse that lumbered around these hills for a thousand thousand years, sometime after the extinction of the dinosaurs. An artist's rendition across the back wall combines the torso of a hippo with the hide of an elephant and a lugubrious wattled head that only a mother brontothere could love. The animal stands in a broad savanna, near the edge of a meandering stream, delicately protruding its loose upper lip to browse on the leaves of a tree.

Again, we are asked to imagine this scene playing out *here*. If the major repository of dinosaur bones lies just south of town, fossils from the Age of Mammals have been discovered in a number of sites to the north, east, and west, all within easy reach of Eastend. Together, these deposits document the epoch immediately following the impact disaster and pick up the story again in the era of the brontotheres. From then on, beginning about forty-five million years before the present and continuing for thirty million more, the record is remarkably rich and continuous. The Calf Creek quarry, straight north of town, for example, has yielded teeth and bones from more than seven dozen mammalian species, including *Hesperocyon gregarius* (the oldest known member of the dog family), tiny bears, ancestral deerlets and pronghorns, camels, rhinos, three kinds of miniature three-toed horses, and two types of giant brontotheres. All are now extinct.

I have to admit that I didn't get all these facts straight on my first visit—there was too much oddity to absorb at once. In fact, even after several subsequent tours, I still wasn't sure that I understood what I was being told, so one day I stopped to chat with the center's paleontologist-in-residence, Tim Tokaryk. A big guy ("ex-football," he explains), he occupies a cramped office just around the corner from the gift shop. Everything about his space—from the portrait of Darwin on the door to the shelves of learned volumes that crowd the walls—speaks of his dedication to science. What will he think of me if I ask him what I really want to know? Is it possible that the land around us remembers?

I watch Tim for signs of discomfort when I blurt out this embarrassing query, but he merely nods his head. "Within an hour's drive of town, I can hit almost a continuous seventy-five million years of vertebrate history," he says matter-of-factly, "from the end of the Western Interior Seaway, through the Late Cretaceous and the extinction event, all the way to the Age of Mammals and the emergence of the grasslands. If you want a wonderful, wild, and wicked story about the past and the present, this is the place to come. We have to realize that we're the luckiest."

AFTER IMBIBING as much evolutionary excitement as we can handle, Keith and I often pause on the walkway outside the T.rex Centre to take in the view. See, just down below, there's our little house on the edge of town, with its proud new window, its apple tree, and its tidy chain-link fence. Back in the everyday world, the monstrous procession of life and death on display in the T.rex Centre fades into fantasy, as if it were a kind of scientifically sanctified freak show. And so it remained until one day, a few months after our arrival in Eastend, when the here and now cracked open, and cracked me open, too, and the profound strangeness of the real world crept under my skin.

We were out walking on the flat benchlands above the center—Keith and I, the dogs, and our grownup daughter, who had joined us for a few days. It was stinking hot, mid-August, so when we noticed the shimmer of water on a cutaway bank down below, we made a beeline for it, the dogs panting in the vanguard. In they all went, humans and canines alike, and no one else seemed to notice that the pond was green and slimy, with an oozy, muddy bottom that sucked up between your toes. As I watched my ankles disappear into the muck, I realized that there were worse fates than being hot. Surely, I thought, someone should sit up on the shore and watch the dogs, in case one of them tried to run off.

At first, all the bathers were happy to lie in the water, but after a while, one pesky dachshund (oh, they are wonderful trouble those dogs!) developed serious wanderlust. After retrieving her several times, I plopped myself down in the dirt, red faced and streaming with sweat. I had had it. So when the darn dog took off yet again, I found myself appealing in desperation to the fairies, the genius loci, the lares and penates, to whatever powers might be listening, to see if I could cut a deal. If I went after the runaway one more time, the world had to agree to show me something special.

With this illusory prospect in mind, I mustered the strength to stagger to my feet, as the dog tripped lightly up a scabby little erosion channel, heading for parts unknown. "I'm on your tail, mutt," I muttered as I closed in on her rear. "And, this time, you're going on your leash." But even as I attended to these practicalities, I kept scanning my surroundings, nurturing my heat-hazed hope. We'd cut a deal, hadn't we? I'd done my part—dog in hand—so where was my reward? In the ooze down below, where my family was still lolling? On these scabrous cutbanks or in this dried-up watercourse? It looked like I'd been skunked. Then, just as I was on the verge of returning to normalcy, I noticed something odd. A rock was poking out of the edge of the path, quite unlike anything else around. It was lumpy, gray-white, and ugly, about the size of my head. Idly, I wrestled it out of the earth and flipped it bottom-side up.

In an instant, I had forgotten about being put-upon and overheated. "You guys," I shouted, as I hurried my companions out of the swamp. "You've got to come see this!"

We crouched in a circle around the rock, intent as children. There, protruding from the dry underside of a dry rock in a prairie gulch was a perfect fossilized clam. The hills had begun to show us their secrets.

{FOUR}

RAVENSCRAG ROAD

"No frontier is marked between the
Western landscape and a country of fable."
BERNARD DEVOTO, *Mark Twain's America*, 1932

LTHOUGH KEITH and I usually traveled to Eastend on our own, with our rabble of pets, we were always glad when friends or family paid us a visit. The pleasures of these hills were so abundant that there was plenty to go around, and we were eager to share our house with like-minded souls. Our most frequent guests were our daughters, one of whom had stood in the magic circle around the fossil shell, and the other of whom joined the party whenever she was able. It was this second daughter—a bright, practical soul, not given to morbid thoughts—who made an observation that ever since has echoed through my mind. She came into the house one morning, after a walk with the dogs, and said that the hills seemed sad to her. "It feels like something bad must have happened here."

"Sad? Something bad?" I objected. "But it's so peaceful. So lyrical." Hadn't she heard the pair of orioles chanting to one another at their nest? Hadn't she seen their miraculous silken basket swaying from a cottonwood branch? Hadn't she noticed the way the morning light was slanting down the valley, filling it to the brim?

She nodded in vague agreement, but her eyes were already skidding past me to gaze out the window at the river hills. "Maybe it's just the sense that so much has been happening here for so long. It's kind of spooky."

And I have to admit that she is right: this land is filled with ghosts. Sometimes, especially when Keith and I are settling in for one of our long summer stays, I wake up to find myself troubled by an unaccountable melancholy. It lodges behind my breastbone, a dull, lumpen ache. That's when I, too, find myself staring out at the river hills and thinking about my own ghosts. That's when I think about my mother. She died of cancer on a beautiful day in June, and it wasn't until after she was gone that I began to understand how the view from my window, and the hills beyond, connected me with her.

That summer was a season of endings. My mother's death was echoed a few weeks later by the closing-out auction at my grandparents' farm south of Hanna, Alberta, a place I knew from her stories and from the few awkward visits we made there during my childhood. In recent years, I'd been trying to get her to go back with me, though she had been hard to convince. Once, we made it to the closest town but, with a mere three miles to go, we lost the scent—couldn't find the right road, too much had changed, she said—and after that she refused to try again. "Why would you want to go there?" one of my uncles asked. The place was being farmed by its owners-in-waiting, the local Hutterite colony, while the last of the Humphreys, my once dashing uncle, cowered inside the beat-up house, drinking himself to an early death.

And then my uncle was gone, and my mother, and the farm and all of its accoutrements—rows of rusty, disabled equipment set out at the foot of the ramshackle yard—were up for grabs by the highest bidder. What the Stegners had achieved in less than a decade had taken us a hundred years, yet here we were, at the end of days, in "our own special plot of failure."[1]

When my mother was dying, I know that she often returned to her childhood home in her thoughts. "I never told you very much about my mother," she'd say, and this time it wasn't the witch who had tried to give her away to a neighbor that she needed to talk about. "All those babies, one after another, with no running water." She paused, as if the very thought made her weary. "It must have been hell on earth."

Standing in the weedy, dissolute farmyard on auction day, I'm glad that my mother isn't here to see strangers picking over the bones of her parents' life work. But there is one thing that I know would have raised her spirits, as it raises mine. Beyond the array of old junk, past the reach of the auctioneer's babble, across the stubble fields, along the horizon, sprawls a mottled, low-slung ridge. I know at once, as if by instinct, that what I am seeing is the Hand Hills, where my child-mother used to pick saskatoon berries and where she had once been threatened with groping, or worse, by a neighbor. "Dad," she had shrieked, "Dad," and her father had emerged from the berry bushes in time to rescue her. Although the hills had been erased from my memory—who knew that they were visible from the yard?—their presence must have lodged in my body when I visited as a child. I'd seen them again without knowing it when we arrived in Eastend and opened our house to them. The hills outside our window were the motherland.

AND SO off Keith and I set to court this other expanse of prairie and this other range of hills, more intent than ever on understanding where we were. As the circuit of our explorations broadened, we traveled with the road map in hand, one person as driver and the other as navigator. But even with this guidance, we often ended up flying by the seat of our pants, not entirely lost but pleasantly off the map. As long as we kept to the pavement, we usually knew where we were, but the instant a side road beckoned, luring us onto a dirt track and then to a rutted trail, jogging right, then left, then right, across a ford, past a farmyard, up and over a hill— well, who really needed to know exactly where we were? I still have the handwritten diagram of one of those early journeys, studded with exclamation points ("tall larkspurs, southeast slope, probably saline!" "4 wild boars!!" "a moose with a newborn calf, right out on the open prairie, way up on the top of a hill!!!") and glossed with cheerful expressions of doubt ("somewhere," "eventually," "a bit confused here").

Yet it was surprising how quickly we began to learn our way around. For one thing, even counting the dirt tracks and goat trails that we favored, there weren't actually many roads. Unlike the flatlands of the surrounding plains, with their mile-by-mile grid, the rumpled rise and fall of the hills had curtailed the road builders' ambitions. For the most part, traffic was directed along coulees and river valleys or around the foot of the hills, making the dendritic web of connections relatively easy to learn.

It also helped that our travels were rich in surprises and small adventures, each of which was charted on our mental maps. You see that scrubby field beside the highway? It may not look like much, but that's where a certain C. Savage was eaten alive by mosquitoes when she dared to venture through a glittering expanse of wild sunflowers. And that house, screened behind a windbreak just north of the Claydon grid, is not just any house. It's where our new friends Bob and Betty live with their troupe of eight wire-haired dachshunds. A mile or so to the south lies the ditch (twenty telephone poles from the corner) where we once found an injured ferruginous hawk—an endangered species—and called the conservation officer in Shaunavon who drove twenty-five miles to help, only to discover that the bird was too badly injured and had to be put to death. Week by week, month by month, the landscape was filling up with the sediment of our experiences.

OF ALL the trips that we have made around Eastend, my all-time, number-one favorite is a short jaunt to the west, to a place that was once a place but that now doesn't really exist. The hamlet of Ravenscrag, fourteen miles distant, formerly enjoyed all the amenities of rural life—three grain elevators, church and school, a pool hall, and a ladies' baseball team—but the last forty years have reduced it first to a ghost town and then to a plot of vacant lots that, today, serve as a staging ground for a large private farming operation. Yet through all these changes, the site has kept its charm. Like Eastend, Ravenscrag sits on the broad lap of the Frenchman Valley, encircled by unruly, misshapen hills. Looking at them, you could be forgiven for wondering if, long ago, a company of gargantuan green camels had stretched out to rest in a disorderly heap, all shoulders, noses, and knees, never again to rise from their stony dreams.

The most spectacular pleasure of this landscape, however, lies neither at Ravenscrag nor at Eastend but about halfway in between. Here, the hills on either side of the valley are drawn subtly together to define a broad-floored, walled-in trench. On the flatlands at the bottom, the river continues its drowsy meanders, leaving just enough space along its southern margin for a gravel road to scoot past. Up above, on both sides of the valley but especially to the north, steep, dissected cutbanks rise to clip the horizon, enclosing a river of sky. You could come this way a hundred times and catch these embankments in a hundred different moods, sometimes towering and majestic, sometimes hazy and withdrawn, sometimes outlined with snow so that their bones show.

But the rewards of this passage are not merely scenic; they can also be revelatory. During the research for my prairie book, I'd picked up a copy of something called *Field Trip Guidebook No. 6*, "Upper Cretaceous and Tertiary Stratigraphy and Paleontology of Southern Saskatchewan," a slim volume that had been prepared for the post-conference delectation of visiting scientists in 1997. Despite its unpromising title and technical vocabulary—any bets on the nature of a "neoplagiaulacid" or a "polarity chron"?—the book turned out to be a little treasure. Almost the entire volume focused on the Cypress Hills, including the eroded headlands along the Ravenscrag road.

Granted, I missed many of the finer points under discussion, since a lot of it was over my head, but there was no mistaking the essence of what was being said. It seemed that the saga of the earth's history, the same stupendous story we had encountered in technicolor at the T.rex Centre, could also be read in the subtle earth tones of the valley between Ravenscrag and Eastend. According to the guidebook, the

strata that were exposed there dated back some eighty million years, to the gray mudstones and siltstones that had
formed on the bed of the Bearpaw Sea. (My mind flashed
to the fossil clam, embedded in dark, fine-grained stone.
Eighty million years ago: was it possible?) After that salty
beginning, successive chapters were written in successive
striations of grayish-yellow, milk white, mauve, greenish-
brown, charcoal, gray, and tan, each bearing witness to an
episode in the earth's long turmoil. The final retreat of salt
water. The fallout from distant volcanoes. The emergence
of Scotty and Co. The thin stratum of disaster. The swampy
forests of the early Age of Mammals.

With *Guidebook No. 6* at my elbow, I summarized these
teachings in my notebook as a simple, handwritten chart.
The next time we headed for Ravenscrag, I took the page
along, hopeful that it would enable me to decipher the strata
for myself. But apart from the most obvious features—the
chalky extrusions of the Whitemud Formation and the sev-
enty meters of ancient lake bottom that formed the face of
Ravenscrag Butte—I was still at a loss. All the same, I felt
honored to sit on the roadside and contemplate this record
of the creation of the earth, even if I wasn't able to decipher
it chapter and verse.

Come to think of it, there was another feature—or the
absence of a feature, really—that I *was* able to discern. The
guidebook described what it called an "unconformity" at
the very top of the cliffs. Apparently, after millions of years
of archiving everything that happened by collecting sedi-
ments, the landscape had eventually been subjected to
erosion by water and wind, with the result that a thousand
meters of soil had been stripped from the surface. (How
these folks could estimate the depth of the land that was
missing by studying what remained was one of the fine

points that escaped me.) As a result of this downgrading, there was a chronological break, or "hiatus," between the sandstones of the Ravenscrag Formation (the second layer from the top) and the surface that overlaid them. With the aid of binoculars, I could see that the cliffs were surmounted in places by what the field guide identified as the Cypress Hills Formation, a coarse jumble of stones that had washed out of the young Rocky Mountains and been carried eastward and northeastward by great, gnashing rivers during the Miocene era. The disconnect between the Ravenscrag and Cypress Hills formations represented an erasure of about thirty million years. In other places, the round, river-washed stones were missing, and the banks were topped with debris and silt that had been dropped just a few thousand years ago by the retreating glaciers.

Yet to an unschooled eye, nothing looked amiss; one layer overlaid another in complete innocence. Apparently, an unconformity could exist between the present and what we knew of the past, and very few of us would ever notice it.

ACCORDING TO *Guidebook No. 6,* the whole of the Cypress Hills country, including the uplands along the Ravenscrag road, are an "erosional remnant" of a landscape that originally covered the surrounding plains. If the hills now stand hundreds of meters above the prairies, then hundreds of meters of earth must have been stripped away from everywhere else. I once buttonholed a geologist and asked him how something so inconceivable could have happened and where all the lost land had gone. He just shrugged and said that, in theory at least, it had either been carried north to the Arctic Ocean, via the creeks and rivers of the Saskatchewan drainage, or south to the Gulf of Mexico, through the Frenchman and the Missouri river system. That was probably why the hills had survived as hills, he said, because they lie midway between the two oceans, on the divide between major watersheds, and thus have been spared the full, relentless force of erosion.

Through erosion, the land forgets. And perhaps it was all this talk of remembering and forgetting that sent my thoughts tumbling back to Wallace Stegner again. I was staring out the window one day, idly wondering if that bump on the horizon had been laid down before or after the final retreat of the Bearpaw Sea, when it occurred to me that Stegner had been engaged in a kind of literary and historical stratigraphy. As he compared the heroic myth of the pioneer era with the equivocal data of his own childhood, he had detected evidence of unconformities, gaps between the received version of the settlement story and the reality he had lived. Part of his purpose in writing *Wolf Willow*, I suspected, was to take a stand against this erasure—to backfill the legend with truth.

What had he written in? First, failure: "the inevitable warp, as hope was the woof, of that belated frontier."[2] Second, deprivation: "A dull, dull little town," he says of the Eastend he encountered in the 1950s, "where nothing passes but the wind, a town so starved for excitement that a man's misfortune in losing his false teeth in the river can enliven a whole winter's poolroom and hardware-store conversation."[3] Finally, his mother's painful disappointment: "For her sake I have regretted that miserable homestead, and blamed my father for the blind and ignorant lemming-impulse that brought us to it."[4] It must have been hell on earth.

WHO WOULD have suspected that learning to read the geological strata along the Ravenscrag road, in a halting

beginner's way, would have helped me to perceive new layers of meaning in Stegner's revisionist history? Yet even as
my insight into *Wolf Willow* deepened and my respect for
its author grew, there was still something about the book,
something I couldn't quite put my finger on, that left me
feeling bad tempered. I'd read the first few chapters with
fascination, and then my mind would begin to skid and I'd
find myself hot and bothered, fast-forwarding to the end. At
first, I thought my grievance was with the concluding pages,
in which Stegner denounces virtually the entire population of Eastend as a bunch of losers who stayed here because
they weren't smart enough to leave and who are doomed to
the eternal boredom of a "stagnant peasant society."[5] As
a product of a rural "peasant" society, and on behalf of my
growing circle of Eastend friends, I felt like taking *Wolf Willow* and chucking it at him. Thank you so very much, Sir
Tooty Snooty Stanford Professor.

But, no, that couldn't really be the problem, because I'd
managed to read that part of the book. It's when I turn to the
second section that, *wham*, I run into a wall. Here, under the
banner of "Preparation for a Civilization," Stegner focuses
on the prelude to Western settlement, events in which he
and I, though a generation apart, have a vital interest. The
story he has to tell is not a pretty one. By his account, the
settler society of the twentieth, and now twenty-first, century lies unconformably on a raw and savage past.

"However it may have seemed to the people who founded
it," he writes, "Whitemud [a.k.a. Eastend] was not a beginning, not a new thing, but a stage in a long historical process.

"Seldom, anywhere, have historical changes occurred so
fast. From grizzlies, buffalo, and Indians still only half possessed of the horse and gun, the historical parabola to Dust

Bowl and near-depopulation covered only about sixty years. Here was the Plains frontier in a capsule, condensed into the life of a reasonably long-lived man."[6]

In his determination to counter the effects of erosion, Stegner has penned a kind of thinking man's Western, starring the Cypress Hills as a land that had been lost for millennia in the great vastness between two river systems. Admitted to history by the belated arrival of explorers (Captain John Palliser in 1859) and traders (a Hudson's Bay Company man named Isaac Cowie in 1871), this innocent and previously unpeopled landscape unwittingly provides a stage for a final, violent reiteration of the frontier tragedy. The story is bloody, from the war-club-wielding warriors who, according to Stegner, had whooped through the hills for generations, to the officially sanctioned brutality of the American armed forces during the Indian Wars of the late 1800s. ("No one who has studied western history can cling to the belief that the Nazis invented genocide," Stegner notes grimly.)[7] It is a chronicle of ecological catastrophe, beginning with the ruin of the abundant animal life that once occupied the hills—"Beaver heaven, elk heaven, bear heaven, buffalo heaven," shot to smithereens—and culminating in the calamity that inevitably befell the people whose lives had depended on wild things.[8]

"Within little more than a decade, fur traders, *métis,* and Indians would find their whole world collapsing under them," Stegner laments, "the buffalo would be all but gone"—pause for a moment of silence; cue the swelling music—"and law and order in a red coat would be patrolling the coulees where a few years before hardly any man, red or white or halfway between, would have dared to go."[9]

Lay on the truth telling, Mr. Stegner. I can handle that. But could you please keep a damper on that tone of triumph?

And do I detect just the slightest tincture of racial prejudice in your remarks?

Here we have a brilliant man, a scholar with the soul of a poet, a master storyteller, and a person who has dedicated himself to speaking the painful truth, yet even he had been hornswoggled by the march-of-progress myth. What if the hills weren't really an uncharted wilderness before the Europeans showed up? What if there was more to the indigenous prairie cultures than whooping and war clubs? What if it wasn't the Métis (as Stegner claims) who stripped these hills of wildlife, bringing their own way of life to an end? What if the red-coated heroes of the North-West Mounted Police hadn't always managed to live up to their Dudley Do-Right reputations?

For the agricultural settlement of the western plains to rank as "progress," the new order had to be an improvement on what had been here before. Try telling that to the grizzly bears, Mr. Stegner, to the elk and the buffalo. Try telling that to Chief Nekaneet, walking through the snow.

Interview with Wallace Stegner, Pulitzer Prize–winning author, spare bedroom/office, Taylor House, Eastend, SK, July 30, 2010, 11:33 AM

C.S.: Good morning, Mr. Stegner, er, Wallace. May I call you Wallace?

W.S.: If this is about Eastend, you'd better make it Mr. Page.

C.S.: Right. Mr. Page, let me get straight to the point. I was shocked by some of the things you say in *Wolf Willow.* Like here, on page 65. [She picks up the book and reads.] "The more Indian the *métis,* the more insatiable their desire for drink."[10] Or over here, [she flips back a few pages] you write about "an Indianism as savage as that of the most unregenerate Blackfoot,"[11] and later on you refer to the people who took refuge in the Cypress Hills in the 1870s and 1880s as an "ethnic junk heap."[12]

You're an open-hearted and humane man, or so you lead us to believe. But do you remember what Thoreau said about "a charity that hides a multitude of sins"?[13] How could you say such disturbing and, I have to say it, racist things?

MR. P.: [He takes his glasses off, places them on the table, and rubs his eyes wearily.] Yes, in retrospect, I can see that I could and should have aspired to a larger humanity. In my own defense, I can only say that I am a product of the culture that formed me, a dung-heeled sagebrush town on the disappearing edge of nowhere.[14] And kindly remember that I have been dead now for almost twenty years. If anyone has a right to be an anachronism, surely I do.

C.S.: When I was a kid, I used to imagine my grandma and an Indian woman (we didn't have other words then, just Indian) standing across from one another, on opposite sides of a field, just frozen there, unable even to shout out a greeting.

MR. P.: [He puts his glasses back on, raises his head, and nods.] About once a year in my boyhood, a family or two in a rickety democrat wagon would come down to Eastend from somewhere and camp for a few days in the river brush. I remember packs of us hanging wary as coyotes, just out of what we imagined was gunshot range, around their camps, spying on the dark children, the shapeless women, the heavy-featured men with braids and (we felt) a shiftless mixture of white and Indian clothes. We watched the whole

outfit as we would have watched ugly and perhaps dangerous animals from a blind. The moment an adult emerged
from one of the brush shanties we edged back, prepared to
scatter.

[He pauses.] Sometimes we yelled catcalls in their direction, half in derision and half speculatively, to see what
would happen. Nothing ever did. With what I now recognize
was either helplessness or dignity they ignored us, and any
temptation we might have had to go on into the camps and
hobnob with their kids was discouraged by the dogs and by
our mothers' warnings.[15] That was the end of it.

C.S.: You're gone now, so you're the perfect person to answer
this next question. Is it fair to judge the dead for thinking
what they thought and for doing what they did? Can the
dead avoid censure by claiming to have been captives of the
culture that they inhabited?

MR. P.: I can only speak for myself, Miss Whoever-You-Are,
and I can honestly say that I struggled against intolerance
for as long as I lived. Now, you'll have to excuse me. It is too
late for any of this.

WOLF WILLOW is a very personal book, and its gifts of can-
dor, intelligence, and lyrical beauty are testaments to the
generosity and talents of one gifted man. The book's blind
spots, by contrast, are societal. In publishing *Wolf Willow*,
Stegner was speaking to and for his demographic, trying to
make sense of what it meant to have participated, as bare-
footed kids at the turn of another century, in the grand
scheme of Western development. If he failed to detect the
racist underpinnings of the Great Plains adventure—the
confident assertion of white European superiority and

the unquestioned value of European "civilization"—he certainly wasn't alone. As for his easy capitulation to the "growth-and-progress gospels" that, in his heart of hearts, he recognized as frauds, he clearly deserved to be outed as a backslider. But perhaps he also rates a vote of thanks for beginning to chip away at the dogmas of historical certainty.

With these issues out on the table, I'm finally able to put my misgivings behind me and open my mind to the book. In particular, I become interested in the stratigraphy, or periodization, of Stegner's narrative, which I recognize (partly from incessant repetitions in elementary school) as the classic structure of Western historical writing. The story begins, as it always does, with the primordial silence of prehistory and then advances through the successive, sometimes overlapping, stages of exploration, fur trade, open-range ranching, frontier disorder, and the eventual dawning of law and "enlightenment." The boldest, blackest line of demarcation is inscribed in the final stages of this process, between the outlaw West of the 1870s and 1880s and the bucolic landscape of farm and village that emerged in its wake.

In *Wolf Willow,* Stegner absolutely insists on this division, chronicling not only the decimation of the buffalo but also what he describes as the complete obliteration of the indigenous peoples. "The white man literally created the culture of the Plains Indians by bringing them the horse and the gun," he writes, "and just as surely, by conquest, disease, trade rum, and the destruction of the buffalo, he doomed what he had created." [16] As for the Métis, he says that their only legacy was "death and emptiness." [17] The buffalo prairie and its people had apparently gone extinct, as dead as the dinosaurs. And just as, in ancient times, the mammals had moved in to fill the vacancy left by their reptilian antecedents, so the incoming settlers were pictured flowing into a vacant land, obeying the dictates of the survival of the fittest.

Fine and dandy except, of course, that's not really what happened. The indigenous civilizations of the Great Plains did not die out in the nineteenth century, whether the "frontier" had ended or not. They were present when the settlers arrived, and they are fiercely alive right now. So why have the keepers of Western history, including friend Wallace, been so obsessed with defining the end of the old, indigenous West?

Since I have the advantage of a historian-in-residence, I decide to put the question to him. Keith and I are sitting in the backyard on a blustery day in mid-summer, lunching on hummus and beer. "I get the impression that they are trying to draw a line between the past and the present," I say, between mouthfuls. "It's like they want to distance it, to disconnect us from something."

Keith picks up his glass and looks at me thoughtfully. "There are a lot of things that nobody talks about," he responds, after a pause, "in the imposition of colonial power."

What lay inside that obscure stratum marked "end of the frontier"? Was it true that something terrible really had happened here?

FIVE

STONE CIRCLES

Everything the Power of the World does is done in a circle.
LAKOTA ELDER BLACK ELK, *Black Elk Speaks*, 1932

BY THE time I'd settled my score with *Wolf Willow*, a couple of years had passed, and life and work had been moving along, ordered and full of purpose. Then, as another winter closed down around us and just as I was preparing to write the last chapter in my prairie book, something terrible happened to us. Keith was diagnosed with cancer. Unable to foresee the three years of treatment that would follow or his eventual recovery, we were jittery, brittle with anxiety.

For Keith and me in this time of crisis, Eastend and its circle of hills offered a respite not just from the city but also from the wonderful, terrible technologies—the wheezing scanners, the cold sizzle of radiation, the monstrous hypodermics—that were busily saving Keith's life. Naturally, all of our worries came with us when we hit the highway, and sometimes the deserted streets and empty rooms that greeted us on our arrival threatened to make things worse.

Our thoughts echoed in our minds and in the small-town silence: *Don't die, don't die, don't die.* But then something would happen to break the spell and draw us back out into the light.

For instance, we might be sitting at the kitchen table and look up just in time to see, right there in front of us, a tiny round bird with big round eyes and a spangle of red atop its head, feeding in the pine tree at the front of our house. It couldn't be, but there it was, a ruby-crowned kinglet, a spectacular little number that is typically found far to the north and west but that has a pinpoint distribution right here in the Cypress Hills. And now, we were among the lucky few who had seen it.

Or we'd take the dogs for a walk in some scuffed-up, dung-strewn patch of pasture on the outskirts of town, heads down, wrangling dachshunds or preoccupied by our own thoughts, until one of us caught a flicker of movement under the thin thatch of grass. "You've got to see this," a voice rings out, and then we're both down on our hands and knees, watching a bizarre creepy-crawly with the body of an ant, the hairy integument of a woolly bear caterpillar, and the red-and-black warning coloration of something poisonous, hurrying from wherever it was to wherever it wants to be. Back at the house, we Google "red black hairy ant" and discover that what we've seen is a kind of wasp with a sting so powerful that people only half-jokingly have dubbed it the "cow killer."

A marshy seep beside a broken-down bridge yields a ground-hugging patch of gentians the color of winter twilight. Small sinks in the course of a summer-dry gully are studded with shooting stars and blue-eyed grass, flowers so precisely formed and so perfect that they could have been crafted out of porcelain. Ruby-red strawberries glisten in the grass, condensing the sweetness of summer into a morsel the size of one's littlest fingernail. Through all the long, trying months of Keith's treatment and subsequent recovery, the hills repeatedly offered us these small moments of beauty and surprise, quietly distracting us from our troubles and suffusing every cell in our bodies with a species of joy. One or both of us might be dying, but for the moment, we were alive.

Denn alles Fleisch es ist wie Gras, und alle Herrlichkeit des Menschen wie des Grases Blumen.[1] All flesh is like grass, and all loveliness is like a flower in the field.

Was there ever such a country for empathy with our frailty?

IT IS a characteristic of the prairies that things hide in plain view. Think of pronghorns, for example. For all their gracile runner's build, they are substantial animals, comparable in height and weight to Great Danes or female mountain goats. Yet seen at any distance, a herd of pronghorns looks strangely insubstantial, as if they were caramel-colored exhalations of the caramel-colored grass. (It's amazing what several million years of evolutionary coexistence can accomplish!) I've been known to laugh out loud when a blotchy, whitish boulder resting in a field suddenly raises its head and fixes me with its dark eyes. *That ain't no rock, ma'am. That there's an antelope.* It's enough to make you wonder what you've been smoking. The prairie's hallucinatory powers seem to be strongest when clouds settle low over the curve of the land, and the light is caught, shimmering, between earth and heaven. In the gloaming, a jackrabbit standing against the sky looms as big as a deer, and the ground-nesting birds that leap up at your feet almost immediately vanish into the dazzle. It was on one of those strange twilit days that Keith and I stumbled across something half hidden in the grass that was to give my travels in the hills a sharp new focus.

We were walking our dogs on the north bench of the Frenchman Valley, upslope from the T.rex Centre, twenty minutes or so from our house, following a route that we had taken dozens of times before. If we'd been in the mood, we could have dropped in to visit the fossil clamshell in a' coulee a short hike below, but the weather was brisk—a perfect day for striking out across the high tablelands that line the valley. So away we went, shouldering into the wind, our words blown from our mouths in tatters, our heads and eyes turned down. The earth beneath our feet was covered with a Persian carpet of ground-hugging vegetation, no more than ankle high: a finely knotted fabric of selaginella, or club moss, fringed with *Artemisia frigida* (silver sage), and tufted with the curly leaf blades and dainty eyelash-shaped seed heads of *Bouteloua gracilis,* blue grama grass.

The whole place was strewn with rocks, rocks, and more rocks, all river rounded and smooth, as if they had been flung from fast-moving water onto this arid shore. In a sense, of course, that is exactly what happened, since these cobbles are a manifestation of the Cypress Hills Formation (last seen atop the cliffs along the Ravenscrag road) and were carried here by mighty rivers thirty or forty million years ago. No wonder the rocks are blotched and crusted with lichens; even at a rate of millimeters per year, they've had time to grow. No wonder the stones are strewn about at random, dropped wherever Miocene rivers and, much later, Ice Age glaciers happened to leave them. There is no rhyme or reason to these deposits, but that doesn't stop your eye from trying to find a pattern by literally connecting the dots, searching for meaning where none is possible.

And, then—wouldn't you know it?—a hint of order appears. At first, you're sure that you are seeing things, but no, the array of stones that you've stumbled across really does form an arc. See, you can follow it, step by step, all the way back to where you started, a complete circumference. And now that you know what you're looking for, you quickly locate half a dozen more rings clustered round about, each set apart from its neighbors at a companionable distance. Some of the circles are drawn with single rows of rocks, while others are framed by two or more stones laid side by side, so they seem to form a narrow path. Walking on these eloquent relics is like walking the spiral pathways of a labyrinth.

Apparently, the play of light and shadow on that particular day had allowed us to detect a phenomenon that had previously been hidden from view. Although Keith and I had seen tipi rings before, we had never found any for ourselves. Now here we were, the proud "discoverers" of the tracings of a small encampment. Since then, we have had the good fortune to trip across dozens of similar rings along the Frenchman and in other places round about, including a large and well-documented site in Chambery Coulee, overlooking the T. rex quarry. (As one of our new Eastend area acquaintances once commented, evincing more pleasure at the thought than her choice of words denotes, "This whole part of the country is infested" with stone circles.) But no matter how many times the experience is repeated, there's nothing like a first kiss, and the impact of that very first time has never faded.

I've lost count of the number of times we've been back to visit that spectral village since we first encountered it. Part of the wonder of the place is the precarious chance of its survival, on a fringe of natural prairie bordered on the south by the drop of the valley and on the north by a straggly stand of cultivated grass. If the farmer had made even two or three more rounds with his plow, the whole site would have been lost and the stones would have ended up, sans stories, in anonymous rock piles. It is thanks to the thin soil and uneven ground along the valley rim that these stone circles were spared from destruction.

The special charm of the site lies in its location on a bench overlooking the modern town, as if daring you not to make the connection between *then* and *now*. Standing in the center of the largest circle, where the fire would have been, I try to imagine the people who lived here for an unknown span of days at some unknown time in the past. Were they here two centuries ago or two millennia? I find myself straining to hear fragments of their conversation, their laughter, the barking of their dogs, but all I hear is the wind and the great silence.

And then I'm eight years old again and standing on the road that cuts across the Indian Quarter on my father's father's farm. In my mind's eye, I see my grandmother and the buckskin-clad princess just as I had left them all those years ago, still facing each other, mute and immobile, across an empty field. I'm reminded of picnicking by the Beaverlodge River, thinking of the disappeared encampments and of the people who had lived in them. Now we were here, having a good time, and they were . . . well, the best I could say was that they were somewhere else.

By settling in Eastend, Keith and I had unwittingly gained intimate access to the past, not only to the stupendous grotesqueries of evolution and earth history but also, as the tipi rings made clear, to the more recent, domestic experiences of people. So here I was, a mortal being; a wide-eyed traveler in a country that knew more tales than a mere human could ever tell, a dislocated child who longed for an attic full of old stories, a disgruntled adult who smelled a rat in the accepted version of the homestead saga, and a writer at the end of her big *Prairie* project, with the prospect of time on her hands.

An intention began to form in my mind, hazy at first, like a cryptic boulder-that-could-be-an-animal seen from afar but becoming clear as time advanced. I would find out who these stone people were, learn what had become of them, and see how their story intersected with the myth of agricultural settlement. I'd pry open the locked wooden chest labeled "1870–1885, End of the Frontier" and reveal whatever moldy, disagreeable truths were stored within.

If I had wanted a reason for being in Eastend, I now had one. *My mission, should I choose to accept it.* Had I suspected how much I had to learn or how painful the truth can be, I might have set the project aside and gone on to other things. Even without that foreknowledge, I harbored certain doubts. What if I wasn't the right person to do this work? After all, I was just a visitor here, a glorified tourist really. Who was I to muck around with local history? More troubling still, I am the descendant of incoming settlers, with no filial link to the people who had made the tipi rings. Was it disrespectful, or just plain wrong, for me to attempt to address their history?

But even as I wrestled with these misgivings, that first vague impulse to proceed was coalescing into a plan. And I was encouraged by what, logically, must have been mere happenstance. It was another monochrome, overcast day, and this time we had driven up onto the north bench and parked our truck on the edge of a dirt track that parallels the valley rim. Our plan was to hike the few hundred yards cross-country to the edge of the bank, pause and take in the view, and then proceed toward the headland where the tipi rings were. At first, everything was perfectly ordinary, and we scuffed along, *oohing* and *aahing* over plants, rocks, lichens, the spiral ascent of a hawk. Then, just as we rounded the last curve, almost in sight of our goal, we were stopped in our tracks by a voice that seemed to come out of nowhere. And again—a throaty, mournful song, punctuated by high-pitched yips.

"What was that?"

"A coyote?"

"Look. I think it's straight ahead."

Against the silvered sky, a silvery shape raised its muzzle and uttered a tremulous howl.

"Isn't that where the tipi rings are? It has to be sitting right in the middle of them."

Calling our dogs close beside us, for the coyote's safety and their own, we continued slowly forward, not at all sure what would happen. The coyote watched us advance for a minute and then retreated to the top of the next rise, far enough away for comfort but still in plain sight. When we moved, the coyote moved; when we stopped, it stopped up ahead and sang, for all the world as if it were trying to tell us something. This continued for the better part of an hour, until we'd finished our walk. When we finally turned our backs on the valley and headed for our vehicle, the coyote sat down on its haunches and watched us retreat, its quavering notes continuing to bridge the gap in between.

In all likelihood, we had encountered a juvenile member of the species *Canis latrans,* still behaviorally naïve, which had vocalized in response to the novel stimulus of our activities. Strange to say, however, that's not how it felt. Instead, I had an eerie sense that the land was speaking to us, calling us yet again to pay attention.

BACK AT my desk in the city, I settled down to learn as much as I could about the stone circles. As always with a new quest, my first step was to make a sweep through all of the available sources—books, articles, websites, videos, whatever I could find—looking for anything and everything that might have a bearing on my subject. The goal is, as quickly as possible, to catch a glimpse of the big picture, figure out who's who and what happened when, and generally get myself oriented. It's a bit like constructing a mental map of a landscape when you first encounter it, the way Keith and I had done in our early days in Eastend.

Almost immediately, I found myself entangled in a dense thicket of words. It took me a while, for example, to figure out that the term "Blackfoot" could refer to either a single nation, the Siksika, or more generally to the member nations of the Niitsítapi, or Blackfoot-speaking peoples, a group that includes the Siksika (Blackfoot), the Káínai (Bloods), and the Piikáni (both the North Peigan of Alberta and the South Peigan, or Blackfeet, of Montana). What's more, the Niitsítapi alliance formerly included the A-a-ni-nin, a people who are also known as the Atsina or Gros Ventre. At times the Niitsítapi were at peace with the Ktunaxa, or Kootenais, who migrated with the seasons from the mountains onto the plains. At other times (particularly times of hunger), these nations faced each other as enemies. The same was true of the Niitsítapi's relationship with the Nakoda, or Assiniboines, and the Nehiyawak, or Cree, two allied groups who had expanded westward and northwestward onto the plains by the 1600s. Adding to the remarkable cultural scene on the northern plains were the Yankton and Plains Sioux, also known respectively as the Dakota and the Lakota. And, of course, by the eighteenth century, there were also the half-breeds, or Métis people.

It was like entering an unknown country, and it left my mind in a spin. But sometimes, in the midst of the confusion, my research turned up a gem. That was the case with a story, first published in 1901, under the title of "Little Friend Coyote."[2] I wish I could tell you exactly when and where this story was first recorded, but unfortunately the text doesn't say. I'm guessing northern Montana, in the mid- to late 1800s. All we know is that the story was told "by the flickering fire in [a] Blackfoot skin-lodge" by an unnamed elder (probably a member of the Piikáni nation) and that it was written down, with the aid of an unnamed translator, by an amateur ethnographer from New York City named George Bird Grinnell. If a photographer had been present, he'd have captured a huddle of figures seated around a luminous spire of smoke and the glint of a steel nib scratching away in a notebook.

Grinnell understood the importance of recording the stories as accurately as he could. "As the Indians have no written characters," he noted, "memorable events are retained only in the minds of the people, and are handed down by the elders to their children, and by these again transmitted to their children, so passing from generation to generation."

"Until recent years," Grinnell continued, "one of the sacred duties of certain elders of the tribes was the handing down of these histories to their successors. As they repeated them, they impressed upon the hearer the importance of remembering the stories precisely as told, and of telling them again exactly as he had received them, neither adding nor taking away anything. Thus early taught his duty, each listener strove to perform it, and to impress on those whom he in turn instructed a similar obligation."

So here is the story as nearly as possible as Grinnell recorded it. One summer when the Siksika (Blackfoot) and Piikáni (South Peigan) people were camped together, a young Blackfoot man named Front Wolf and a Peigan woman named Su-yé-sai-pi met, married, and decided to settle with the Peigan camp. Unhappily for Su-yé-sai-pi, however, her new husband was a natural leader and was often away from home on one expedition or another. So when he announced that he was going to visit his parents, Su-yé-sai-pi, who had been lonely during his absence, insisted on going along. Front Wolf tried to dissuade her—"The distance is great," he told her, "and there is danger on the way." Her parents were worried too, but Su-yé-sai-pi just laughed and began to prepare for the journey.

"At this time," the storyteller continues, "the Peigan were hunting on the Lower Milk River, but the morning that Front Wolf and his wife started away the whole camp moved too, for the chiefs wished to pass the hot season along the foothills of the great mountains. At the last moment five young Blackfoot men, visitors in the camp, decided that they too would return home, so they set forth with the couple and helped drive the little herd of horses that Front Wolf intended to give his relatives.

"The northern tribe was thought to be summering on the Red Deer River, and a course was roughly taken for the place where it joins the Saskatchewan. This brought the little party, after three or four days' travel, to the Cypress Hills, or, as they were named by the Indians, the Gap-in-the-Middle Hills.

"They reached the southern slopes of the low buttes one morning, after being without water all the preceding day, and prepared to camp and rest at the edge of a little grove, close to which a large, clear spring bubbled up from a pile of sunken boulders. They did not know that a large camp of Kutenais was just behind the hills where they stopped, and that one of their hunters, seeing them coming, had hurried home and spread the news. Su-yé-sai-pi had scarcely started a fire when the warriors from the camp were seen to be approaching the little party from all directions, completely hemming them in. Although these two tribes, the Blackfeet and Kutenais had once been very friendly to each other, they were now at war."

And so it happened, somewhere on the south slope of the Cypress Hills, that Front Wolf and his five companions were killed, and Su-yé-sai-pi, the sole survivor, was taken into captivity. Who knows what fate would have awaited her had it not been for an elderly widow who, filled with pity by the girl's plight, supplied her with provisions and advised her to escape into the night? Pursued by scouts, tormented by thirst, the young woman hid wherever she could, once spending an entire day deep in an old wolf den. When night fell, she climbed out to search for water, wandering this way and that, "and when daylight again brightened the sky, found herself at the place where her husband lay. Yes, there lay the bodies of Front Wolf and his friends, now shapeless and terrible things. And the Kutenais had vanished.

"Worn out from her long tramp, and nearly crazed from thirst, the poor woman had barely strength to go on to the spring, where she drank long of the cool water, and then fell asleep.

"The sun was hot, but Su-yé-sai-pi slept on. Well on in the afternoon she was awakened by something nudging her side. 'They have found me,' she said to herself, shivering with terror, 'and when I move a knife will be thrust in my side.' She lay motionless a little while, and then could bear the suspense no longer; slowly rising up and turning back her robe, what should she find lying by her side but a coyote, looking up into her face and wagging his tail!

"'Oh, little wolf!' she cried. 'Oh, little brother! Have pity on me. You know the wide plains; lead me to my people, for my husband is killed, and I am lost.'

"The little animal kept wagging his tail, and when she arose and went again to the spring, he followed her. She drank, and then ate a little dried meat, not forgetting to give him some, which he hastily devoured. She talked to him all the time, telling him what had happened, and what she wished to do; and he seemed to understand, for when she started to leave the spring he bounded on ahead, often stopping and looking back, as much as to say, 'Come on; this is the way.'

"They were passing through the broken hills [the Cypress Hills], and the coyote, quite a long way ahead, had climbed to the top of a low butte and looked cautiously over it, when he turned, ran back part way, and then circled off to the right. Su-yé-sai-pi was frightened, thinking he had sighted the Kutenais, and she ran after him as fast as she could go.

"He led her to the top of another hill, and then, looking away along the ridge, she saw that he had led her around a band of grizzly bears, feeding and playing on the steep slope. Then she knew for certain that he was to be trusted, and she told him to keep a long way ahead, to look over the country from every rise of ground, and to warn her if he saw anything suspicious.

"This he did. He would wait for her at the top of a ridge, where they would sit and rest awhile, and as soon as she was ready to go on he would run to the top of the next rise before she had taken fifty steps. If thirsty, she would tell him, and in a little while he would always take her to some water. Sometimes it would be a small trickling stream in a coulée; sometimes a soft, damp gravel-bed, where she was obliged to scoop out a hole; sometimes it was a muddy buffalo-wallow—and it was always strong with alkali—but it was the best there was."

In this way "little friend coyote" led Su-yé-sai-pi all the way from the Cypress Hills to her own people on the east slope of the Rocky Mountains. There, aware that the camp dogs would kill him given a chance, she reluctantly bade him farewell. But she promised that, whenever the camp moved, she and her family would depart last, so that they could leave food for him.

"And often," the anonymous elder tells us, "as Su-yé-sai-pi and her people started on after the others, they saw him standing on a near hill, watching them out of sight."

That other coyote had stood on a hill and watched Keith and me out of sight as we left the tipi rings. Where had little friend coyote been trying to lead me?

SIX

CHIMNEY COULEE

The antelope mourns the buffalo in the night.
CORB LUND, "The Truth Comes Out," 2005

WHO WERE the stone people and what had become of them? Although I was born and raised on the prairies, had read prairie authors and studied prairie ecology, it was remarkable how little I knew. The mystery of the stone circles exposed my ignorance of the deep human story of the Cypress Hills and of my home territory in general.

Fortunately, thanks to my sweep through the library, I had acquired a stack of scholarly papers on northern plains archaeology. They confirmed that the tipi dwellers had lived by hunting buffalo (I had been pretty sure about that) and that all the sites Keith and I had found were old and possibly ancient. The earliest known stone circles on the Canadian prairies were created between four thousand and five thousand years ago, making them as evocative in their own quiet way as the standing stones of Britain or the pyramids of Egypt, with which they are roughly contemporary. The

majority of the rings that have so far been studied, however, date from the last two thousand years. This means that
when Jesus was born and when Nero fiddled while Rome
burned and when the Maya were building their temples
in Mesoamerica, people were using these stones to secure
their shelters against the wind, both here in the Cypress
Hills and across the broad heartland of North America. A
conservative estimate puts the number of surviving stone
circles in southern Alberta alone at more than a million.

Unfortunately, you can't tell how old a tipi ring is just by
looking at it. Although the buildup of soil around the stones
and the growth of lichens are often suggestive, the only way
to get an exact fix is by unearthing shards of bone and sending them off for radiocarbon analysis, an option far beyond
the means of casual investigation. The sites that Keith and I
discovered might have lain there for decades or centuries or
millennia, but we would never know for sure. And perhaps,
in the end, it didn't really matter. Taken together, these
abandoned campsites represented an ancestral human
habitation that extended from the late nineteenth century
back to the invention of the tipi and even beyond, to the
retreat of the glaciers. Ten thousand years of hunting and
gathering, of births and deaths, of hard work and repose.
Ten thousand years of continuity, adaptation, and survival.
Although the physical traces the people left were often subtle, their perennially renewed presence on the landscape
was a monument in itself and put my four generations of
proud belonging into a humbling new perspective.

MOST OF what I know about tipi rings comes courtesy of
University of Calgary archaeologist Gerald A. Oetelaar, who
in 2003 published a long, lucid, blissfully readable article
that might have been entitled "Almost Everything You Ever

Wanted to Know about Stone Circles." (Instead, it was sent out into the world under the drab banner of "Tipi Rings and Alberta Archaeology: A Brief Overview.") If you've ever wondered about the size of an average ring or the number of tipis per camp or the reason some rings are single while others are outlined with a double row of stones, then Professor Oetelaar is the person to turn to. His answers, in case you are curious, are as follows:

SIZE: Tipi rings range from 2.5 to 9 paces (or yards) in diameter. The size differential is thought to reflect differences in family size, wealth, and status. The old theory that small rings date from the time of the dog-drawn travois, with the larger ones reflecting the hauling power of the horse, is no longer accepted. Very large stone circles (more than 9 yards in diameter) are interpreted as ceremonial structures.

NUMBER: A typical site contains the traces of between one and four homes, each with room to sleep, on average, about eight people. Camps of up to one hundred tipis, with space for hundreds of inhabitants, have also been documented.

CONSTRUCTION: Single rings with sparsely spaced stones are thought to have been used for brief stopovers in summer. When excavated, they generally yield very few artifacts. By contrast, heavily built circles, with double rows or closely packed stones, are thought to represent long-term winter encampments and are typically much richer repositories of artifacts and, hence, of information.

What is the most promising place to look for tipi rings? Oetelaar has an answer for that as well. Although there's a chance of finding stone circles wherever the grasslands have survived in a natural state, the prospects are best along the banks of major rivers and in isolated uplands. One notable case in point is the Cypress Hills.

As evidence, Oetelaar cites a survey conducted in the 1990s by an archaeologist named Alison Landals, who with two colleagues mapped all the tipi rings along a 250-mile stretch of a soon-to-be-constructed oil pipeline. Beginning at the wonderfully named Wild Horse border crossing on the Alberta-Montana line, she and her companions walked north, crossing the westernmost slope of the hills, all the way to central Alberta. From the outset, the trek was pleasantly eventful, with discoveries along the way, but things really got exciting when the researchers began the ascent into hill country. Suddenly, instead of occasional, scattered findings, they encountered dozens of circles each day, far more than anywhere else on their journey. In addition, many of the campsites in the hills were heavily loaded with stone—as much as a ton of rock per tent—an indication that they may have been extended winter residences. (This impression was strengthened by test excavations that yielded a rich store of mementos, including bone shards, stone tools, and fire-cracked rock from hearths.) If every campsite along the route had been marked with a point of light, the Cypress Hills would have lit up like a beacon.

Who would have dared to imagine that a landscape capable of recalling the epic of geological creation and the travails of extinct beasts would also conserve an important chapter in the history of our own species?

THE SPECIAL magic of archaeology lies in its ability to take oddments of abandoned, long-forgotten debris and infuse these mundane objects with meaning. The tipi ring sites in the Cypress Hills, for instance, are not just mute circles of rocks. To an archaeologist, they speak of the long-term importance of this region as a place of sustenance. For countless generations, the hills have provided water in a dry land, firewood on the otherwise treeless plains, and, on their westernmost heights, the only stands of lodgepole pines (for tipi poles) for hundreds of miles in any direction. In summer, the coulees offered glistening harvests of berries and sources of medicinal plants; in winter, they provided shelter not only for people but also for animals, including the all-important buffalo. *Otapanihowin,* the Cree called them, a word that translates as "livelihood" or "the means of survival." Even in times of severe adversity—during decades and occasionally whole centuries when the plains were scorched with drought—the hills provided a refuge for the two-legged, the four-legged, the winged ones, and the plants.

How they must have loved this place, those resilient people, with its sudden drops and its long vistas, with the glint of the little river coiling down below. As people who were fed by the land, did they sense the vitality of the wild earth pulsing through their veins? Did they know, beyond any need for conscious knowing, that they were another name for the grass and the wind and the snow? These questions were beyond the reach of archaeology or any certain knowledge, though that didn't keep me from wondering.

Despite the best that science had to offer, the people who once lived inside the stone circles remained inscrutable. What languages had they spoken? Where had they and their descendants gone? The answers, if any existed, were not to be found at my desk. It was time to hit the road again and see what stories the land itself could be persuaded to tell.

EARLY ON, I'd picked up a tourist map of Eastend and environs, a simple photocopied sheet with one side devoted to the attractions of the town—among them, the Wallace Stegner House, the T.rex Discovery Centre, and Charlie's Lunch (ice cream!)—and the other detailing points of interest in the surrounding country. Two of the latter in particular had caught my attention. The first, labeled "Crazy Horse Camp," was on the near end of the Ravenscrag road, a ten-minute drive from our house. "Legend has it," the map caption read, "that Chief Crazy Horse and a group of his followers camped here in 1876." Crazy Horse, the great warrior and the leader of the Lakota resistance? And 1876—wasn't that the summer when the Lakota and their allies had defeated the golden-haired General Custer ("Old Curly" to his troops) near the Greasy Grass River? I had a dim recollection that, in addition to that engagement, Crazy Horse had been involved in several other costly battles with U.S. forces in succeeding months and that he had been killed, in government custody, the following autumn. Had he really found time to slip across the border and slip back again, in time to keep his appointment with history?

Given the number of times that Keith and I had traveled the Ravenscrag road, I'm surprised that we hadn't stopped earlier to check out the Crazy Horse site. But there it was, just where the map had promised, marked both by a small signboard and by an arrow that gestured to the northwest, across the river flats. If the powers-that-be had gone to this much trouble to draw attention to the place, maybe there really was something to the Crazy Horse story. So off we set with high hopes, clambering over tussocks and through tangles of potentilla, looking for whatever might remain of the historic encampment. Instead, an hour of searching yielded an abundance of cow pies and a scatter of rocks but nothing that bore the signature of a Lakota presence.

It wasn't until months later that a friend (one of those invaluable small-town people who have the inside dope on everyone and everything) explained that we'd been misled. Apparently, there really is a large campsite, with dozens of tipi rings and the outline of what might have been a ceremonial lodge, but it is up on the rim of the valley, several miles from the signage and the dot on the map. If you stand at the information point and squint in a northwesterly direction, you can more or less make out the approximate location. "But don't you go up there and look for it," our friend warned. "The site is on private land and the landowner takes a mighty dim view of trespassers."

So that was that. Maybe the Lakota had visited here and maybe they had not. Wherever they were, I bet they weren't blithering about oneness with nature, I thought, suddenly embarrassed by my earlier flights of romanticism. I bet they were angry and desperately sad. How had it felt to become a trespasser in your own homeland?

FORTUNATELY, THERE was another location on the visitors' map that looked more promising. It bore the alliterative name of Chimney Coulee, and to get there we turned our backs on Crazy Horse hill and headed east, via the main drag, to the outskirts of town. An immediate left turn took us north along the voluptuous margin of yet another wide, light-filled valley. (And to think that people have the nerve to say the prairies are boring!) Five minutes later, we drew up in a grassy lay-by and, with the inevitable escort of dogs, proceeded on foot along a dirt path toward a three-paneled sign, much larger and more impressive than the one at the purported Crazy Horse site. With luck, its enhanced dignity signaled an enhanced intent to divulge the whole truth and nothing but.

The air that day was tangy with sage and bright with the shimmer of aspens that crowded around the kiosk. Pools of flattened grass showed where deer had bedded down in the shelter of the signboards. A few steps farther along the path, someone had provided a picnic table, now half-buried in thistles, and erected a squat stone cairn, presumably as a supplementary source of information. Beyond the cairn, the footpath forked, with one branch swinging invitingly up a grassy slope to the left and the other plunging straight down into a dark, spruce-filled chasm. It wasn't so much a coulee as a miniature canyon. Down there the air was cool and green, scented by evergreens and alive with the bright *dee-dee*'s of forest birds. This place seemed to have everything, the best of two ecological worlds.

Over the years, we've visited Chimney Coulee so often that I'm no longer sure exactly what happened when. But I do know that this is where I first heard the rasping sigh of a nighthawk's wings cutting through the sky as the bird performed its undulating aerial courtship dance on a spring evening. Experiences like that were pure prairie. When we headed into the ravine, by contrast, we were instantly transported to what might have been a hidden valley in the Rockies. Once, for instance, we were hiking on one of the paths that tunnel along the course of the canyon, struggling over deadfall and through prickly underbrush, when we happened upon a series of muddy wallows. What was that musky smell? And who or what had left those large cloven prints deeply impressed in the muck? Just as we were putting two and two together—autumn, rutting pits, bulls, the most dangerous animals in the forest—something up ahead grunted and huffed in a menacing way, and we scrambled out of there in a hurry.

Bull moose, deer, nighthawks, bluebirds, glittering beetles feeding on purple vetch: there was always something on offer at Chimney Coulee. But if the land was resplendent with life, the narrative on the signboards could have been written in blood. This lovely place had witnessed an apocalypse.

AS SOON as I read the first sentence on the kiosk, I realized that I'd encountered this story before, during my apprenticeship with *Wolf Willow*. (Apparently, there was no getting away from Mr. Stegner.) "In the winter of 1871–72," the text began, "Isaac Cowie established a Hudson's Bay Company trading post in this coulee." I glanced around the quiet site, trying to imagine log buildings, stacks of baled furs, the hustle and bustle of people going about their work. Did any of them feel a prickling at the back of the neck, an uneasy sense that all hell was about to descend upon them? The year before Cowie arrived, the HBC had sold its vast holdings of western lands to the British Crown and thence to the infant Dominion of Canada. In far-off Ottawa, back rooms were filled with fat talk about a transcontinental railroad that would link the country from coast to coast and service the anticipated onrush of settlers. In the ledgers of the new nation, the buffalo ecosystem was already being written down for obliteration.

In the few short months of his occupation that winter, Cowie acquired the hides of 750 grizzly bears and 1,500 elk, with as many more going to other traders in the area. And hides were only a sideline of his operation. His real interest

was acquiring buffalo meat that, made into pemmican, pro-
visioned the company's posts and brigades in the northern
forest. When it came time to pack out in the spring and head
for Fort Qu'Appelle, Cowie had amassed so much meat that
he couldn't squeeze all of it into his fleet of carts. Forty carcasses—more than eleven tons dressed weight—had to be left
behind to rot or be scavenged.

Eleven tons of carrion. Fifteen hundred elk. And 750
pathetic slaughtered bears. Of the latter, Cowie would one
day write, "Most of these were unprime summer bearskins—
mere hides which every hunter was using for cart covers
instead of the ordinary buffalo bull hides, for large numbers
had been slain off horseback in a run on the prairie. Many
of them were of immense size approaching that of a polar
bear; one skin measured by me was thirteen feet from tip to
tail. This natural reservation of the grizzly and the elk soon
ceased to harbour them . . . owing to [the consequences of]
our invasion."[1]

During the next ten years, the entire Great Plains, from
western Canada south to Texas, would become a slaughter-
house. The foundation for agricultural settlement was being
laid in wholesale carnage.

IN THE Middle Ages, scholars often kept human skulls in
their libraries as objects of contemplation. They served as
memento mori, bleak reminders of the human life span.
On my desk at the moment in continuation of this tradition, I have the partial remains of a buffalo cranium, a
lifeless reminder of the power of commodity markets to
wreak havoc. The right eye socket of the skull is broken, the
entire snout is gone, and the top of the skull is open, reveal-
ing a honeycomb-like pattern of interior reinforcements.
On either edge of the shattered face, the horns sweep out

to the sides, their surfaces as ridged and rough as if they were made of coral. *Those are pearls that were his eyes.*[2] This relic actually belongs to my friend Mary, who lives at the town end of Chimney Coulee road, on a bend of the French-man River. She was out in her kayak one day when she saw a large object underwater, on the bank below her house, and reached out to capture it.

"I was excited when I saw it," she remembers. "It looked so big. But I sort of wish I had never disturbed it now. Once I got it out, I discovered that it was a crayfish apartment house, with someone at home in every compartment."

Deprived of this purpose, the skull's one good eye socket stares at me blindly, and I find myself longing to reclothe its bones in flesh. Imagine the great shaggy head, the massive shoulders and tapered hindquarters, the ridiculous fly-swat tail. Once conjured, the phantom stands impatiently between my desk and the piano, striking the floor with its hooves, waiting for me to open the door and let it loose. If one buffalo were magically to reappear on the Great Plains every minute, nonstop round the clock, it would take almost sixty years to restore the population to its historic numbers. According to the best available estimates, the Great Plains were once home to more than thirty million buffalo. Within a decade of Cowie's stopover at Chimney Coulee, however, that number would be reduced by 99.993 percent. By the mid-1880s, there were about two hundred survivors on the continent, in half a dozen shattered groups. The last wild herds in Canada, and the last subsistence hunts, occurred on the rich pasturelands of the Cypress Hills.

The near-extinction of the buffalo is an oft-told tale but, judging from the current global status of wild species, one from which little has been learned. Instead, we prefer to pass over the tragedy lightly, with phrases like "after the buffalo disappeared" and "when the buffalo vanished," as if the animals had wandered peacefully into the great beyond. This wording has become standard in prairie histories and memoirs—with *Wolf Willow* as a notable exception, to Stegner's enormous credit—and I never encounter such euphemisms without a pang of distress. It's bad enough to know that the buffalo were slaughtered in the name of profit and progress. It's worse to know that, collectively, we have shrugged off our duty to grieve this tragedy.

As an outpost of the pemmican trade, Isaac Cowie's occupation of Chimney Coulee played a role, albeit a minor one, in this destruction. By the 1860s, the Hudson's Bay Company was drawing a total of 106.5 tons of pemmican out of the northern plains each year, almost twice as much as it had required a decade earlier. Watching the long trains of Red River carts heading east, heavily laden with robes and meat, some Native people concluded that the prairies were being tapped to provide sustenance for the entire white populations of North America, England, and France. When a visitor attempted to convince them otherwise, they remained suspicious. "Where then," they asked, "does all the pemmican go to that you take away in your boats and in your carts?"[3]

In the spring of 1872, when Cowie and his teamsters were preparing to depart from Chimney Coulee with their groaning loads, the slopes around the HBC outpost were tense with suspicion. For some time, the traders had been aware that a party of South Peigan, or Piikáni, defenders was in the area, keeping armed watch on their every move. "We tried to open communication with these scouts, by signals," Cowie reports in his memoir, "to which they only replied by signs of hostility and derision, mocking us with flashes from their little round mirrors."[4] Clearly, the Piikáni warriors were in no mood for compromise or discussion.

From my reading, I know some things that Cowie may not have known about the Piikáni people's circumstances that winter. Over the preceding months, their community had been hit by a series of traumas. The first, in the winter of 1869–70, was an outbreak of smallpox that killed one-third of the people it touched. The second, on January 23, 1870, was the massacre by the U.S. 2nd Regiment of 173 people on the Marias River, just across the border in northern Montana. Dispatched to exact revenge for an earlier fracas over stolen horses, Major Eugene M. Baker (a notorious drunk) had led his forces in a predawn attack on the wrong camp of people. In the hectic confusion that followed, the cavalry suffered one casualty, when a soldier fell from his horse. Since the men of the camp were out hunting that day, most of the Piikáni people who died were elders, women, and children.

These were heartbreaking losses and, nearly 150 years later, are still a cause for grief. More trouble struck a few months later when, on October 24, 1870, a large party of Cree and Nakoda soldiers attacked a Piikáni camp on the Belly River (now the site of Indian Battle Park in Lethbridge, Alberta). Although the engagement ended in a brilliant victory for the Piikáni and their Siksika and Káínai allies, who unbeknownst to the attackers had been camped near at hand, the action claimed the lives of another forty men. The death toll among the Crees and Nakoda approached three hundred.

In the old days, warfare on the prairies had been a kind of lethal sport, in which touching an enemy or stealing his horse counted for almost as much as claiming a scalp or a life. But now, when a noose was tightening around the buffalo and the people who depended on them, when the life-giving herds were contracting year by year in both number and distribution, when thirty million had shrunk to one million, and a weird stillness had fallen on the eastern and southern plains—every skirmish had become a fight to the finish. "Fight on!" a Piikáni chief had exhorted his people, a month after the Baker Massacre. "Fight on, fight on! Go on fighting to the very last man; and let that last man go on fighting too, for it is better to die thus, as a brave man should die, than to live a little time and then . . . starve." [5]

Late in the winter of 1871–72, the struggle came to Chimney Coulee. From the vantage of the surrounding hills, the Piikáni watched as the train of heavily laden carts pulled away to the east and as, a few minutes later, Cowie and another trader followed on horseback. "We had not gone, at a lope, more than a quarter of a mile," Cowie recalled, "when we heard a spluttering volley, evidently from a large party, and by the time we reached the carts the smoke, which arose from the site of our wintering houses, proclaimed that the Blackfeet had set them on fire." [6] Nine people—Nakoda from Wood Mountain, who had arrived to scavenge for odds and ends as the traders were packing out—were killed in the melee. Their remains were found by Métis hunters the following summer.

ALL I had wanted to know was who had made the stone circles, and yet here I am instead, surrounded by desperation and the nameless bodies of the dead. Yet if these memories are part of my inheritance as a prairie person, I am determined to accept them as my own. I will let them settle around me quietly, layer after layer, loss upon loss.

Standing by the signboard at Chimney Coulee, I strain my senses to pick up a hint of what is no longer there: the bellowing of buffalo, the hair-raising huff of a bear, an acrid whiff of gunpowder. Instead, the air is sweet with sunlight and dappled by a clean breeze that spangles the poplar leaves. I turn my eyes back to the signboard and pick up the story.

I'm not sure what I expected to happen next, but it certainly wasn't this. In 1873, the year after the Piikáni evicted Isaac Cowie, a group of about sixty Métis families had taken up residence here. Although the Piikáni were no doubt troubled by this intrusion, the struggles of the preceding months had left them reeling and in no position to resist the sudden, determined arrival of an entire settlement. As the Piikáni shifted out onto the buffalo plains of the Bow, the Milk, and the Two Medicine Rivers to the west, the Métis (some of whom were returnees from Cowie's party) rolled in from the east, eager to hunt buffalo in the Cypress Hills and on the surrounding plains.

It's often said, only half jokingly, that the Métis nation was born nine months after the first trader arrived on the shores of Hudson Bay in 1670. As the offspring of Scots, English, and French-Canadian men who married into Native families, the Métis were literally and figuratively the children of the fur trade. Whenever a strong back or a skilled hand was needed, the Métis had been engaged, and it was only natural that they became involved in the pemmican trade. At first, their annual hunting expeditions onto the plains—festive communal excursions of five hundred, then eight hundred, then a thousand or more screeching carts, governed by an agreed-upon code of laws—were staged from Pembina, south of present-day Winnipeg. But as the buffalo herds contracted to the west, it had become impractical to trek across the emptied prairie, *va et vient*. Some families began to stay on the plains for the winter months, as *les hivernants*, and so the settlement at Chimney Coulee was born. In the summer, when they were hunting buffalo, the Métis lived in tipis, like their relatives.

If it had been difficult to imagine this peaceful place as the scene of an armed encounter, it was almost as hard to

picture it, just a few months afterwards, as a lively community of several hundred people. According to the text on the
kiosk, the Métis called their new winter home Chapel Coulee—probably *Coulée de la chapelle*—and it had "consisted of a
Roman Catholic church, a cemetery with six known graves,
and several cabins . . . about 14 feet wide and between
30–40 feet long. They were partitioned every 10–12 feet to
form separate living quarters, each with a stone fireplace
and chimney." When the agricultural settlers arrived in the
area twenty years afterwards, the houses had disappeared
but dozens of the chimneys still stood sentinel.

When the wind sings in the tops of the spruce trees, you
can almost catch the lilt of a Métis fiddler playing the Red
River jig. And when a hawk screams overhead, it recalls the
voices of children racing *sosemanuk,* or snowsnakes, down
the slopes or flying past, shrieking with joy, on their tobog-
gans. But there is little now to remind us of the terrible
winter of 1879–80, when the wind howled around the log
houses and the snow lay in deep drifts and the children were
pale and listless from lack of food. The buffalo ran thin and
scrawny in the Cypress Hills country that summer, and by
autumn they were done. The Métis pulled out of the coulee
that year and never returned.

To Wallace Stegner and other historians of his generation, the Métis were an "unwashed and barbarous" people
who had brought disaster upon their own heads,[7] and there
can be no doubt that the Métis were highly efficient buffalo
hunters. Long before the pemmican trade hit its peak, they
were already delivering more than a million pounds of meat
and hides to Red River in a year. Did their activities contrib-
ute to the extermination of the buffalo from the Canadian
prairies? Yes, of course, it did. But were they responsible
for sponsoring the slaughter or for creating the rapacious

demand for buffalo products or for failing to regulate the hunt? Just as obviously, they were not.

The Métis did not number among the rich and power-ful. They were ordinary *Jeans et Jeannes,* simple people with few material possessions and limited options for earning a living. When one of the *hivernants* acquired a cookstove, complete with tea kettle and frying pans, he instantly became a Big Man. My heart goes out to the young Métis hunter, aged twenty-five and with a family to support, who explained in the mid-1860s that he couldn't stop running buffalo, no matter what the consequences. "I must take my part," he said, "with all the other people who . . . [are] kill-ing buffalo and getting rich."[8] Faced with our own failure to respond to climate change and an extinction crisis that now threatens twenty percent of all amphibians, mammals, and birds, we have little reason to believe that we would have chosen differently or better.

Once the buffalo had been extirpated from the Canadian prairies, the Métis scattered. Some rode south to the Judith Basin of central Montana, where all the buffalo hunters in the world were closing in on the last surviving herds. By 1883, those herds had also been finished, and the buffalo ecosystem was gone. With their way of life shattered, the Métis became peddlers or teamsters or trappers or ranchers or farmers or all of the above, around places like Medicine Hat, Pincher Creek, Edmonton, and Round Prairie. Some dispersed up the North Saskatchewan River, and many—as I was stunned to learn from my reading—made their way to the Peace River Country, the place where my father's fam-ily would settle and where, one day, I would be born. Could it be that those far-distant places and seemingly uncon-nected events were caught in the web of the same forsaken narrative?

{SEVEN}

MODERN TIMES

It wasn't the end of the world ... but you could see it from there.
JAMES WELCH, *The Death of Jim Loney*, 1979

WHAT HAD started as a playful adventure was gradually ratcheting up from whimsy to engagement to full-on obsession. I'd wake in the morning amid the flotsam and jetsam of anxious dreams, wondering what that plane crash or flooded house or lost child was trying to tell me about the Cypress Hills and its ragged histories. What do you want from me? I'd ask the view outside my window. I come from the Peace River Country eight hundred miles from here. Why is it so important for me to listen to all your sad, old, moldy, half-forgotten stories? But in my heart of hearts, I already knew the answer. The stories the hills have to tell are bigger than their pinpoint settings, larger than "X marks the spot" on a map. At different times, in different ways, what happened here also happened everywhere else across the North American plains, from the Llano Estacado to the Grande Prairie. The Cypress Hills are a landscape that connects all the dots and offers its teachings to even the most fretful and unwitting of pilgrims.

MEANWHILE, BACK at Chimney Coulee, nothing much is happening because, these days, nothing ever does. For a place that is so richly endowed with stories, the site has astonishingly little to show for it. If it weren't for the text on the signboards, you would never guess that people had lived here, and died here, in the recent past. Their graves lie unmarked and undetected; their chapel has been lost. Even the stone chimneys, which stood guard over the abandoned Métis village until 1915, when the last one tumbled down, have entirely disappeared. They were carried away, stone by stone and load after heavy load, by incoming settlers, who (so the local-history book says) used them to pave their patios and to buttress the earthworks of an irrigation dam at Cypress Lake, an hour's drive to the west.

But the land has never forgotten. When archaeologists conducted test excavations at the site in the mid-1990s (with the assistance of an enthusiastic cadre of local volunteers), they uncovered evidence, in the form of stone tools and fire-cracked rocks, to show that people had frequented Chimney Coulee long before the pemmican trade pushed in. Layered above those early and as-yet-undated occupations lie charred timbers from Cowie's trading post—just inches below the grass—together with a generous scattering of seed beads, tea wrappers, bone shards, and fragments of fine china. The excavation also yielded a number of fish scales, reminders of a remarkable lake that once lay in the valley, a quarter of a mile downslope, which sent its waters both north to Hudson Bay and south toward the Gulf of Mexico. Now reduced to a coarse hatching of marsh plants, the lake was drained in 1907 during the pioneer-era frenzy of rail-way construction.

AS IF these weren't enough stories for one little clearing to tell, Chimney Coulee guards another source of buried treasure. In 1877, three years after *les hivernants* took up sea-sonal residence here, the fabled red coats of the North-West Mounted Police established an outpost a few steps up the hill. A photo taken a couple of years after their arrival fea-tures, from back to front, a sky hazed with smoke from a blur of Métis chimneys, a fringe of spruce trees pushing up from the ravine, three low-slung log buildings, and six gents and a dog strung in a rough line across the foreground. Two of the men appear to be hunters, with rifles over their shoul-ders and small game in hand, but the other four are in full Mountie regalia, complete with either pillbox or Dudley Do-Right hat. (As for the dog, I can only say that it looks like a border collie type, black with a white chest, and shows every sign of being affectionate.)

Although the police were here on and off for the next three years, with a garrison of up to ten men, every surface trace of their presence has vanished. Not far underground, however, the archaeologists found the remains of a log structure where the police post had once stood and, as one might perhaps expect of a bachelor roost, an inordinate number and variety of lost buttons.

TO UNDERSTAND what on earth the North-West Mounted Police were doing in a coulee in the middle of nowhere, we have to shift the scene about an hour's drive to the west, to a site on the West Block, or western upland, of the three pla-teaus that form the Cypress Hills. Ever since Keith and I first arrived in Eastend, the National Historic Site at Fort Walsh had been on our must-see list, though complications involving tow trucks had at first prevented us from making the trip. With reliable transport, however, the ninety-minute journey proved to be a breeze, as we spun west through Robsart and Consul (reversing the route that had brought us here from Cody way back when) and then headed north, on gravel, through a weirdly silent world.

At first, the land sloped away into nothingness, as open as the sea, but then tawny swells rose up on either side of the road and ushered us into a well-watered valley of surpassing beauty. Are we there yet? we wondered. But no, apparently not, because a sign directed us left, up and around a crazy set of switchbacks and through a dark enclosure of trees, before spitting us out on top in wide open country. We rolled on for another few minutes, marbles on a tabletop, and then tumbled over the edge of the world into a valley that, until the last moment, was completely hidden from sight.

By now, we were well and truly in the outback, yet here was a parking lot with space for tour buses, an elegant visitors' center, and a paved path that drew the eye to the top of a grassy knoll.

"Come on," I said, grabbing Keith by the arm. "This is going to be fun." A few steps up the path, we found ourselves looking out and over a spectacular sunlit valley framed on the far side by a rise of hills scrawled with stands of spruce. In the center of the scene, with those dark slopes as a backdrop, stood an array of white-roofed buildings surrounded by a tall palisade and defended by a circular guard house. Finally, we had made it to Fort Walsh. Although the original establishment is long gone—it was dismantled in 1883, as I subsequently found out—early photos still exist, and I can report that, feature for feature, it looked quite a bit like this.

Now, with a Red Ensign fluttering over the barracks and the Canadian maple leaf flying high above the open gates, the fort seemed to be encouraging us to take a sunny walk into the past. What harm could there possibly be in that?

BUT FIRST, a brief stop at the visitors' center and a slight change of plans. Fort Walsh could wait, or so said the guy in a Parks Canada uniform who met us at the door, but the bus to a more distant part of the site was ready to go. All aboard. With a wave of the hand, he directed us onto a school bus, and off we went, goodness knew where.

A gravel track led us down into the valley that we had overlooked a few minutes earlier, our bright yellow bug heading directly toward the wooden fortress. "We'll have you back here in about half an hour, and you can tour the place then," the driver called out, as he swung past the palisade, across what he called the parade ground, and up a slope on the other side.

"See those ruts?" he said, pointing out his side window as the bus growled up the hill. "That's what's left of the old trail from Fort Benton, down in Montana. Everything had to be hauled in that way—oxen, you know, covered wagons, ten miles a day. Even the mail—instructions from Ottawa—used to come in through the States."

Dutifully, I peer out the window at the faint, grassed-over tracks that snake across the side hill. And then, with a cough and a shudder, the bus heaves itself onto the summit of a flat-topped ridge where the land is sweet with wild roses and softened by a shining wind and dimpled by a multitude of round depressions. In the valley behind us, old Fort Walsh lies rectangular and abrupt. Here, everything is lyrical and connected. I nudge Keith in the seat beside me: Where had the driver said we were going? Something about

a massacre? It was hard to believe that this road could lead
to anything sinister.

I'm gazing out the window, watching the light play in
the grass, when the bus wheezes to a stop and the driver
proceeds to answer one of my unasked questions. "Buffalo
wallows," he says, with a broad wave of his hand. "Those hol-
lows in the grass there, they were made by buffalo rolling in
the dirt. Protected them from bugs. Must have been a lot of
them. Buffalo, I mean." He pauses and then continues, dead-
pan. "Bugs, too, come to think of it."

"And down below—" He gestures toward the front window,
and I'm startled to discover that we're perched on the edge of
what looks like a precipice. "Down below there, well, this is
a school bus jump, so watch out for the pile of broken buses
and bus parts at the bottom."[1]

Now that he has our attention, and without missing a
beat, he begins to prepare us for what we are about to see.
"You have to tell it the way you hear it," he says, "and this is
what I've heard." The story begins in the winter of 1873 (the
same year the Métis first settled at Chimney Coulee, I note)
when a band of Nakoda people in the Saskatchewan River
country were struck by famine. The buffalo had been scarce
that winter; by February, none could be found, and the distant refuge of the Cypress Hills seemed to offer the only
hope of survival.

The trek across the snow-deep plains was terrible
and long. The travelers ate their horses, their dogs and
parfleches, made broth from bones dug out of the drifts. No
buffalo, no buffalo. A least thirty members of the party died
en route of starvation and cold. It wasn't until the survivors
reached the hills that the buffalo reappeared, and a young
hunter named Cuwiknak eyaku, or The Man Who Took the
Coat, had the honor of making the first kill. Spring found

the band camped in the valley down below us, at the conflu-
ence of Whitemud Coulee and Battle Creek, recovering their
strength, visiting with friends who had shown up to join
them, and doing a little trading.

There were two traders in the valley that winter, our
driver continued, all trace of jocularity now banished from
his voice. Two Americans, Abe Farwell and Moses Solomon,
both operating out of Fort Benton and both offering a wide
array of goods. "Anything the Indians wanted," that was
their stock in trade: kettles, axes, ammunition, textiles,
beads, and, of course, booze. "Whiskey wasn't the largest
part of the trade, but it was the most profitable." There was
money to be made in the illegal sale of firewater.

Liquor had always been part of the fur trade, the matter-
of-fact voice went on, though traditionally it had been used
in moderation. In the long run, the enterprise had nothing
to gain from murder and mayhem. By the 1870s, however,
the long run had run out. There was only now, with no
tomorrow, and the prospect of a quick buck. This was the
situation on May 31, 1873, when a party of wolfers—rough-
necks who made their living by lacing buffalo meat with
strychnine and skinning the wolves that came to the poisoned bait—rode up to Farwell's post. They'd been on their
way from the aptly named Fort Whoop-up (a center of the
whiskey trade in what is now southern Alberta) to Fort Benton, to cash in on their winter's take of around ten thousand
pelts when someone made off with their herd of horses. Had
Abe Farwell seen or heard anything about those no-good,
horse-thieving Injuns?

Farwell couldn't help them, but why didn't the wolfers spend the night, come in and raise a glass? That night
and the next morning, almost everybody fell to drinking:
the Nakodas, the new arrivals, the two traders and their

employees, even some of the Métis teamsters who had been hired to pack out Farwell's winter trade. The whole place was tipsy, teetering; tempers were on edge. Nothing good could come of this.

HAVING BROUGHT his tale to this point of crisis, our driver falls silent, revs the engine, and rolls the bus over the brink, onto what turns out to be a steep but perfectly serviceable road into the valley. At the bottom, I climb out of the vehicle with trepidation, unsure what to expect, only to find myself beside a crystalline brook, encircled by sunlit hills, in the most benign and picturesque setting one could imagine. Our guide, meanwhile, is intent on continuing his story by showing us the lay of the land. See that willow-fringed meadow, bordered by an arc of the stream? That's where the Nakodas were camped in their buffalo-hide tipis. The two log buildings on the site, one nearby and the other partially visible through the bushes across the creek, represent the whiskey posts where Messrs. Solomon and Farwell, respectively, conducted their business. And so the scene was set for terror.

The trouble began around noon on June 1, 1873, when one of Farwell's men got in a drunken tizzy about a "stolen" horse. Although the animal was quickly recovered—it had just wandered off—voices were raised, shots were fired, and things flared from bad to worse. While some of the traders looked on in horror, others (led by two hard-case wolfers, John Evans and Tom Hardwick, who later became a Montana sheriff) rushed out with their repeating rifles to take cover in the bushes and fire into the Nakoda camp. Undone by adulterated drink, armed only with muskets and arrows, the Nakoda were unable to defend their exposed position. "What had looked for a while like a battle," our guide said quietly, "soon became a horrible massacre." By day's end, the violence had claimed the lives of one wolfer (a French-Canadian named Ed LeGrace) and somewhere between fifteen and eighty Nakodas, a variance that obscures the fate of many women, children, infants, and elders.

When the guns finally fell silent, the attackers swarmed the Nakoda campsite, helping themselves to anything of value and setting fire to the rest. In one lodge, they came upon Hunkajuka, or Little Soldier, the chief who, a few weeks earlier, had led his people across the plains to the safety of the hills. One of the wolfers raised his rifle and shot Hunkajuka at point-blank range, while another busily mutilated the corpse of an old man named Wankantu, and yet another rounded up five women and took them captive. That night four of the women were raped repeatedly inside Solomon's trading post, while the severed head of Wankantu looked mutely down from the top of a lodgepole in the smoldering Nakoda camp.

The fifth woman, a teenager, was spared the same fate as the others through the courage of Horse Guard, Abe Farwell's seventeen-year-old Crow wife, who marched over to Solomon's fort, pistol in hand, and demanded the young woman's release. The rest of the women were held prisoner until morning, when the traders packed up and fled, leaving both posts in flames behind them. As for the Nakoda, many of them headed for Chimney Coulee, at "the end of the mountain," with what little they had left. There the Métis gave them dogs, kettles, and other goods and treated them with kindness. From there, they went on their sorrowful way, aghast at what they had learned about the bitterness of the white intruders.

I can't be sure how much of the story I actually absorbed on that first encounter and how much has sunk in over the years, either on return visits to the site or through reading about it. I can't even be sure exactly what happened after our driver had finished his sorry tale, though I do have a vague recollection of being handed over to a summer student in the red-serge uniform of the North-West Mounted Police, who took us to Farwell's post and did his best to beguile us with the romance of the Wild West. As I recall, there was something about how the whiskey traders doctored their rotgut by flavoring it with tobacco, coloring it with red ink, and even adding strychnine to give it that extra kick. For the most part, however, whatever it was the good "constable" had to say was wasted on a mind still reeling with gunshots and children's screams.

Better to go outdoors. Better to see the flash of warblers in the willows, to smell the spicy aroma of sage, to hear the bright gurgle of the creek as it speeds under the footbridge. Better just to be here and try to accept the solace of this land that refuses to let us forget.

SO THERE you have it, the story of the Cypress Hills Massacre in its essentials, though inevitably there's more to tell. As John Donne almost put it, no story is an island entire of itself; every story is a piece of the continent, a link in an ecology of narrative. For at the same time as chaos was descending on Battle Creek, a separate but ultimately related chain of events was playing out on what might almost have been another planet. Far, far away, across the vastness of the plains and the almost impassible barrier of the Precambrian Shield lay the national capital of Ottawa, and there Prime Minister John A. Macdonald and his grand project of nation building were running into trouble.

One thing had led to another. Building a nation required western settlement; settlement could not proceed without a railroad; the railroad depended on winning elections; winning elections called for funds; funds could be extracted from the fat cats who were competing to build the railroad. Ergo, building a nation meant accepting large sums—some would say bribes—from railway proponents. By the summer of 1873, as the government's financial misdeeds were exposed, Macdonald's ambitious plans for western expansion were in serious hot water.

It was in this context that the prime minister learned, two months after the event, of the spasm of violence in the Cypress Hills. Even before this communiqué reached him, Macdonald's advisers had been pressing him to send an armed force to the plains to establish law and order, keep Native discontent in check, and generally promote the colonization of the country. In fact, Macdonald had already begun to act on this recommendation with the passage, just days before the tragedy in Whitemud Coulee, of an act establishing a paramilitary service to be called the NorthWest Mounted Police. So far, the force existed only on paper, but news of the Cypress Hills atrocities gave the project a political boost. Americans were spilling over the border, threatening Canada's claim to the promised land and bringing their gunslinging racial violence with them. It was time for Canada to act.

Within weeks, a force of 150 red-coated recruits had been dispatched to Manitoba, where they were joined by a second contingent a few months later. Although Macdonald resigned in disgrace midway through this deployment and despite a shambolic march across the plains that nearly ended in disaster, the force arrived in southern Alberta late in 1874 and at Fort Walsh the following summer. The whiskey posts were disbanded, and the police, in concert with the Canadian government, proceeded to do their level best to bring the perpetrators of the Cypress Hills Massacre to justice.

By this time, of course, the malefactors (at least half of whom were technically Canadian) had retreated to Montana, where their many supporters rallied vociferously to their defense: *The Canadian authorities were deluded. The Indians had to be kept under control. No white man should ever stand trial for killing a savage. The wolfers were "the advance guard of civilization." Etc. Etc.*[2] In the end, only three of the accused ever faced charges, and none was convicted. Curiously, however, a rumor spread across the Canadian prairies that the murderers had been severely punished, a belief that burnished the reputation of the red coats and helped them win hearts and minds in the West. Across the line, the U.S. Army was mopping up the last of the "hostiles" and claiming the plains by force. In Canada, the thin ranks of the mounted police were already learning to be more artful.

THE LAST time I returned to the massacre site, that valley of the dead, I came on a very specific mission. Parks Canada had sent a team of archaeologists to reopen and extend an earlier excavation at Farwell's trading post, and members of the public were encouraged to come and help. I'd never been on a dig before, so I was in a cheery mood as a dozen or so of us assembled at the visitors' center and climbed on board the bus for the short, dramatic drive up and over the hogback and down its steep face. The dome of the sky was already hazed with heat when we arrived in the valley—it was going to be blistering hot—and I was relieved when my mentor for the day, a pleasant young archaeology student named Tasha, pointed out a patch of shade inside the reconstructed palisade of Farwell's little fort.

"Here you go," she said, holding out a knapsack filled with the tools of the trade: an assortment of trowels and brushes, a dustpan, a collection of dental picks, and a stylish pair of pull-on pads to protect my knees. Patiently, master to apprentice, she showed me how to measure out a square of dirt and mark it with string so that if we uncovered anything important (or anything at all) its location could be mapped to the last centimeter. "You do it like this," she said, as she picked up a trowel, grasped it at a sharp angle, and scraped away a thin film of earth. "The dirt goes into your dustpan and then you dump it into this pail. We'll run it through a screen later in case we've missed anything."

So *scritch scritch scritch,* I set to work under her watchful eye. After perhaps half an hour of this hypnotic repetition, I uncovered a precious artifact ("Should I pedestal this?" I asked, trying to sound as if I knew what I was talking about), but alas my prize turned out to be an ordinary pebble. Fifteen minutes afterwards, a bent nail appeared. ("Looks recent," Tasha said doubtfully, "but I guess we could bag it.") Lumps of what might have been chinking from a log building surfaced, but it was hard to tell for sure. Then, about two hours and one hand's width below the surface, my trowel bumped against something solid and came up tinged with soot. "Let me see," Tasha ordered. "Yes, I think that's it. That's a charred floorboard from Fort Farwell."

All around us, other teams were also hitting pay dirt in the form of buried sill logs, floor joists, and what might have been fallen timbers from the original palisade. Every discovery spoke to the day, 137 years earlier, when the post had been abandoned in the aftermath of slaughter. Yet none of us seemed troubled by this attribution—I know that I wasn't. Instead, I was having quite a nice time grubbing around in the dirt, chatting with my companion, and enjoying the everyday pleasures of a fine summer morning. Although we were literally in touch with the charred testament of an atrocity, everything that we were doing felt remarkably ordinary.

The boundary between the banal and the momentous is often eerily thin. Kneeling inside Farwell's post, scraping away at the dirt, I found myself remembering a story that I'd read in one of my new favorite books, *Recollections of an Assiniboine Chief*. It was written by the late Dan Kennedy, or Ochankugahe, and published in 1972, a year before its author died, in his nineties. Ochankugahe was born sometime in the 1870s, somewhere in the Cypress Hills, and although he did not witness the massacre, he heard about it at first hand from survivors. What he did see with his own eyes, however, were the signs and symptoms of an even larger and more devastating disaster, and whiskey traders like Farwell again figured in the story.

Unlike the pemmican traders at Chimney Coulee, whose main interest had been in acquiring buffalo meat as a source of food, Montana-based operators like Solomon and Farwell were intent on acquiring buffalo hides as a source of leather. As a result of recent technical innovations at a tannery in far-off Pennsylvania, *otapanihowin,* the peoples' livelihood, had suddenly been transformed into a source of industrial-strength belting material. Henceforth, for as long as the buffalo lasted, the natural capital of the prairie West would literally be used to power the machines and factories of eastern cities. Like Charlie Chaplin's horror-struck little tramp, the buffalo were now trapped in the whirring cogs and wheels of modernization.

Out on the plains, the result was butchery of unparalleled rapacity and rage. The hide hunters hit the southern plains en masse in 1871, and by the time their campaign ended, the southern herd had been shattered. The death toll reached a million buffalo per year and counting, buyers sometimes took in 200,000 hides a day, and block-long stacks of reeking hides awaited the east-bound trains. As U.S. Army Colonel Richard Dodge noted from Kansas in 1873, land that had once been home to "myriads of buffalo" was now strewn with "myriads of carcasses."

"The air was foul with a sickening stench," he wrote, "and the vast plain, which only a short twelvemonth before teemed with animal life, was a dead, solitary, putrid desert."[3]

Mind you, there could be an upside to this picture, depending on your point of view. For as Colonel Dodge himself once cheerfully remarked, "Every dead buffalo is an Indian gone."[4] Another army officer made the point even more explicitly: "Only when the Indian becomes absolutely dependent on us for everything," he said, "will we be able to handle him . . . It seems a more humane thing to kill the buffalo than the Indian, so the buffalo must go."[5] However regrettable the extermination of the southern herd might be, it had to be understood as a necessary phase in the advancement of settlement and civilization.

Of course, young Ochankugahe, the future Dan Kennedy, didn't know anything about these distant developments. He was just a little kid growing up in the Cypress Hills, far away from the main field of slaughter. Although the southern herd had been exterminated, buffalo still persisted in significant numbers on the northwestern plains, and his family was able to live and hunt in their traditional way. But one day, without really knowing what he was seeing, Ochankugahe caught a glimpse of the change that was advancing from the south. "I have every reason to remember the event," Kennedy recollected, but not for the reason that you might expect. What made the day so memorable for him was a skunk bite.[6]

It was a day like any other. Ochankugahe and his family were traveling with a small hunting party (ten or twelve lodges in all) and stopped by a tree-lined creek to spend the night. "The men were watering and tethering the horses and the women were busy pitching camp," he recalled, "but we boys were excited over what we saw a short distance away. There were acres and acres of dead buffalo packed closely together, bloated and rotting in the sun.

"We hurried and made a beeline towards the carcasses," he continued, jumping "from one carcass to another, having the greatest time chasing each other over the hurdles, when suddenly a skunk darted out from one of the carcasses. We gave chase but the skunk beat us to its den. When one boy reached the den, he poked in his arm. I and the others did likewise, but unlike the others, the skunk gave me an unexpected reception. I ran back to camp, howling at the top of my voice, holding my bleeding fingers aloft and wringing them in the air.

"Later that evening as we were eating our supper our elders voiced their indignation and anger at the carnage.

" 'It is the work of Play-ku-tay, the white vandals,' they said."

Throughout the rest of his childhood Ochankugahe wondered what and whom his elders had meant. Then finally, in 1897, he had a chance to put the question to his friend Major Thomas W. Aspdin, a veteran of the North-West Mounted Police.

"I asked him if he knew who the culprits were who had perpetrated this shameless crime, for which we, the Plains Indians, had to endure untold hardships.

"I told the Major of the winter of 1880–81 at Cypress Hills, when we had to eat our horses to survive, and the winter of 1883–84, when five hundred or six hundred of my people [the Nakoda] starved to death at Wolf Point [Montana] because of the ruthless slaughter of the buffalo by Play-ku-tay.

"He listened attentively to my tragic story and must have sensed the bitterness within my soul. I felt certain that, with his experience as an officer of the North-West Mounted Police Force stationed at Fort Walsh and closely associated with the work of maintaining law and order in the West, he should be qualified to know the answer.

" 'Do you know who those buffalo killers were?' he asked and then told me that the 'Play-ku-tay' were sent out by the U.S. Government to starve the Indians into submission."

Staring at the burned floor of Farwell's fort, I knew that whatever the merits of Aspdin's claim, he had glossed over an even more uncomfortable truth. Yes, governments on both sides of the border had been determined to vanquish the buffalo people, to sweep them out of the way. But what had engaged the general population in this project was not a covert conspiracy but the irresistible, amoral pull of what we now call market forces. For the whiskey traders, wolfers, and hide hunters who conducted their business at Farwell's post, the call to destruction had been banal: another day, another dollar, and the gaudy seductions of "civilization."

EIGHT

FORT WALSH

"Le plus terrible dans ce monde,
c'est que chacun à ses raisons."

"The most terrible thing about this world
is that everyone has his reasons."
JEAN RENOIR, *La Règle du jeu*, 1939

IMAGINE THAT we're sitting together on the hillside above Fort Walsh. With every breath, we draw in the winy scent of wild roses, the smoky sweetness of sage, the sheen and shimmer of a perfect summer day. Down below, tourists in shorts and suntops are legging it along the road from the visitors' center to the fort's main gate or climbing aboard the bright yellow bus in front of the stockade. Since the site is only open from the May long weekend until early fall, these days it's always summer at Fort Walsh. If ever there was a place to offer healing and distract us from troubling thoughts, here it is spread out in front of us. In the foreground, a soft screen of wolf willows; in the distance, a rollicking sweep of hills; and in between, on the flats below, a historic site managed exclusively for our edification and pleasure.

It's been years now since Keith and I made our first tour of the fort, and I'm surprised by how much of that visit I can still recall. But then, who could forget the portly gent in full North-West Mounted Police regalia who greets us at the entrance with his knee-high boots polished to a fine luster, his scarlet coat buttoned to the chin, and a white pith helmet affixed to the top of his cranium? The original intention of this uniform had been to mark the mounted police as British, in contrast to the blue-coated Americans, and, in the years when that distinction truly mattered, it had served its purpose well. In deference to this historical significance, our guide bears his domed, beknobbled headgear with all the dignity he can muster.

Despite his cheerfully ridiculous accoutrements, our man knows his stuff, and he quickly fills us in on the basics about Fort Walsh. Although the present-day buildings date from the 1940s, he explains that the original construction was undertaken in 1875 by the thirty-man squad of "B" Division of the North-West Mounted Police, assisted by a crew of Métis sawyers. The commander of the operation was a flamboyant, hot-tempered officer named Inspector (or as he preferred to have it, "Major") James M. Walsh, the man who lent his name to the outpost and whose picture—perhaps we'd noticed?—is featured on the cover of the fort's brochure. Walsh was known to some of his Aboriginal clients as White Forehead Chief, so he must sometimes have worn his pith helmet in the course of his official duties. For this portrait, however, he has replaced his regulation issue with a slouch-brimmed Western hat, which he's garlanded with a scarf and set on his head at a rakish tilt. Done up in fringes and buckskin, with a sword dangling from his belt, Major Walsh exudes a kind of steamy swashbuckling charisma.

It has sometimes been suggested, our guide tells us with a wink and a nod, that Walsh and his men chose this valley on account of the McKays, a prominent Métis family who had settled here several years earlier and who had three marriageable daughters. But the police doubtless had other, more workaday reasons for choosing this location as well—an abundance of flowing water, a ready supply of wood, the promise of shelter from blizzards, and, above all, ready access to evildoers. Despite the atrocities of 1873, whiskey traders were still active in the Cypress Hills, and the police had been sent to put an end to their dirty business.

Once this background has been imparted, our guide indicates with a nod of his helmet that it's time for the tour to begin. What a brutal life it must have been for the men who were stationed here, sleeping on straw-filled pallets in this frigid bunkhouse (there were no winter closures back then), subsisting on an unvarying diet of stew and starches, mucking out a Stygian stable that provided quarters for as many as forty horses. Reveille sounded at 6:30 each morning, announcing a day of rifle drills, artillery drills, riding drills, inspections, patrols, and fatigues that extended until sundown and sometimes beyond. All this for $1 a day for a constable, less for the lower ranks. Small wonder, then, that the site of the enlisted men's barracks has yielded an archaeological treasure trove of bottles that once held beer and various high-alcohol-content patent medicines. Even the higher-ups in the force indulged in illicit drink, though they tried to hide their consumption by tossing the empties down the privy. Like the old joke says, the Mounties had been sent west to keep down alcohol and they sure as heck did their best to fulfill their mission.

By the time we've imbibed all this good-humored scandal, we've made our way three-quarters of the way around the enclosed yard and are sauntering back toward the front gate. Across the lawn, a red-coated guide is shouting commands to a troop of pint-sized police recruits, each outfitted in a tiny scarlet jacket and jaunty pillbox cap. Quick March. Halt. Atten-shun! Nearby, a young sub-constable has nabbed her father and is dragging him off to a mock court, where he is doomed to stand trial for some historical misdemeanor. On all sides, Fort Walsh appears to be delivering on its promise to serve up the past as wholesome family fun. And the grand finale is yet to come.

With a wave of his red-coated arm, our guide directs us through the door of an unassuming log building just to the right of the exit, in the shelter of the stockade. The commissioner's residence, he tells us, and it was here, he says, that the great Lakota chief Sitting Bull—who with his people had taken refuge in Canada following the Battle of the Greasy Grass—once met an official delegation from the United States and sent them home empty-handed. From somewhere, the guide has now produced a sheaf of papers and he's scanning the faces of the visitors who are gathered in the house, looking for volunteers. Who would like to read the words of the American General Terry, as he tries to induce the Lakota to return to the States and settle on their reservations? Who would like to be Sitting Bull and tell the Ugly Americans to beat it?

Most of us hang back shyly, but a couple of brave souls step forward to accept the challenge. Looks like we're in for a touch of drama.

LET'S SAY that you and I are sitting on the hill overlooking Fort Walsh, only it isn't summer now. It is October 16, 1877, around sundown. Below us, the cluster of whitewashed buildings that house the police glows faintly through the dusk; and to the north of the palisade, where a scraggly village has sprung up out of nowhere over the past couple of years, lamps are being lit in the pool hall, the laundry, the restaurant. Somewhere a dog is barking; somewhere a coyote sings its eerie, quavering song. In the distance, a low rumble of hooves and the creaking of wagons announce the imminent arrival of travelers coming in from the south, along the Benton Trail. And then, here they are, breasting the rim of the valley, pausing to take in the view, and proceeding briskly down the slope and across the parade ground toward the fort.

At the head of the procession, two men ride abreast: Colonel James F. Macleod, the commissioner of the mounted police, in his scarlet tunic and gleaming white helmet, and beside him, U.S. Army Brigadier General Alfred H. Terry, resplendent in a blue uniform tinseled with gold braid. These dignitaries are followed by an honor guard of twenty-eight police lancers, their red-and-white pennants fluttering cheerily overhead, and a straggling train of supply wagons, drawn by mules and staffed by a company of American infantrymen. Ordinarily, the U.S. infantry would have been stopped at the border (where three complete companies of cavalry are now waiting to see Terry and his commission safely home) but an exception has been made for the supply train on this special occasion.

No one seems surprised that the Americans have arrived with armed force, while the mounted police get by on chutzpah and an unspoken promise of good governance. Long live the Great White Mother, Victoria Regina, and her worldwide reign of peace and justice.

On one side of the border lies danger; on the other, hope. At least, that's what the Lakota have concluded. And it has been hope, a hope born of desperation, that has drawn some four thousand Lakota refugees across the border into the Great Mother's country in recent months. Behind them lies a bloody saga of mistreatment at the hands of the U.S. government—promises broken, treaty lands stolen (including the sacred Black Hills, "the heart of the people"[1]), peaceful camps attacked. Altogether, it is a record of such iniquity that, in December of 1876, a congressional commission had declared it to be "dishonorable to the nation and disgraceful to those who originated it."[2] But that stinging assessment has gone unnoticed in the national outrage over the events of 26/6/76, the day the Lakota put paid to the 7th Cavalry and its golden-haired commander. Since then, the American military has engaged its superior firepower with redoubled ferocity (even invoking the black-velvet-clad showmanship of Buffalo Bill), forcing some of the Lakota to surrender and accept internment on reservations, while others have fled to sanctuary across the border.

Since their arrival on British soil, the refugees have devoted themselves to hunting buffalo and caring for their children. ("I came here to hunt, nothing bad," Sitting Bull has told the police. "I came to see the English, where we are going to raise a new life."[3]) A few bands have settled temporarily in the remaining buffalo country in and around the Cypress Hills with camps at, among other places, the Head of the Mountain in the west and along the Frenchman River in the east. In response, the police have recently established a small detachment at Chimney Coulee, which they call the East End post, both to surveil the new arrivals and to serve as a stopover on the 120-mile journey from Fort Walsh east to Wood Mountain, where the majority of the refugees have congregated.

That's where Inspector Walsh has had to travel to ask the Lakota if they will come and meet the Americans. The chiefs have agreed with great reluctance. It doesn't help that General Terry was the overall commander of the American forces during the war against the Sioux. It doesn't help that, a day before the Lakota delegation is scheduled to leave for Fort Walsh, a party of around a hundred Nez Perce men, women, and children had struggled into camp, wounded and bleeding, after a calamitous encounter with the American army at the Battle of Bear Paw. These are people who have done everything the white man demanded—accepted the Christian religion, taken up farming, settled in permanent homes—yet in the end they have been evicted from their treaty lands and harried across the country all the way from Oregon.

Even with this painful evidence before them, the Lakota have eventually allowed themselves to be persuaded to attend the parley at Fort Walsh. By the time the general and his entourage enter the stockade, the Lakota delegation is camped nearby. All the leading chiefs are present: Bear's Head; Spotted Eagle; Flying Bird; Whirlwind Bear; Medicine Turns Around; Iron Dog; The Man That Scatters the Bear, with his wife (whose name the clerks at tomorrow's meeting will not bother to note); Little Knife; The Crow; Yellow Dog; and, of course, Sitting Bull. They have come not out of any respect for the Americans or even friendship with the police but in the hope that the Great Mother will see their good intentions and take pity on them. After all, the Dominion government has recently granted a small reserve to Sioux who fled across the border as refugees after the U.S.–Dakota War of 1862. Are not the more recent arrivals equally deserving of consideration?

The meeting convenes at 3 PM on October 17. (For the record, it is held in the orderly room, not the commissioner's house, which won't be built for several months.) Through an interpreter, General Terry lays out the terms of the proposed repatriation: the Lakota will surrender their arms and horses and proceed to the Indian agencies on the Missouri River, where a herd of 650 cattle has been purchased for their use. "From these cows," Terry explains stiffly, "you will be able to raise herds, which will support you and your children . . . long after the game upon which you now depend for subsistence shall have disappeared." In return for accepting this offer and agreeing to live in peace, the general pledges that "what is past shall be forgotten, and . . . you shall be received in the friendly spirit in which the other Indians who have been engaged in hostilities against the United States and have surrendered to its military forces have been received . . . It is time that bloodshed should cease." [4]

Tȟatȟáŋka Íyotake, Sitting Bull, is the first to stand and deliver his rebuke. "I was born and raised in this country with the Red River Half-breeds," he tells the assembly, "and I intend to stop with them . . . You have got ears, and you have got eyes to see with them, and you see how I live with these people. You see me? Here I am!" He pauses to shake hands with Macleod and then with Walsh, before turning back to face the American delegation. "If you think I am a fool, you are a bigger fool than I am. This house is a medicine-house. You come here to tell us lies, but we don't want to hear them . . . Don't you say two more words. Go back home where you came from. This country is mine, and I intend to stay here, and to raise this country full of grown people." [5]

Now comes the part that will never be re-enacted by tourists in the years that lie ahead. Later in the day, after the Americans have withdrawn to their quarters, Macleod holds a private meeting with the Lakota chiefs. Behind closed doors, he tells them that the Queen's government denies their claim to be British and sees them instead as "American Indians . . . who have come to our side of the line for protection." [6] He reminds them that their only hope lies with the buffalo, which will soon be gone, and when that day comes, they can expect "nothing whatever" from the Queen in the way of assistance. In response, Sitting Bull will again grasp Macleod by the hand and express the wistful hope that there will be "lots of buffalo for a long time to come." When he accepts Macleod's gifts of tobacco, provisions, and blankets for the return trip across the plains, he may not immediately understand that, for all her apparent maternal kindness, the Great Mother is cold as stone. He cannot know that, in the corridors of power in faraway Ottawa, the Queen's government has decided to stand by and watch hunger do its work.

MONTH AFTER month ticks past, and the Lakota refugees remain on the Canadian side of the border, with camps in the Cypress Hills (often along the Frenchman near the East End post) and a home base at Wood Mountain. In fact, there are more of them than ever, thanks to a straggling influx of asylum seekers who appeared soon after Terry left, looking for refuge from the misery and political confusion on the American reservations. (These are the people who may have stayed at the purported Crazy Horse camp.) With them, the newcomers have brought word that Crazy Horse, the revered leader of the Lakota resistance, has been murdered, stabbed with bayonets as government officers attempted to put him under arrest. So much for General Terry's promise of forgiveness and friendliness.

Since moving to Grandmother's Country, by contrast, life has been peaceful and good, and the Lakota children have, for the first time in years, begun to play again. But now a familiar enemy is creeping into the camps. After several years of abundance, prairie fires have swept across the Lakota's new country, blackening the grass and keeping the buffalo at a distance. In response, most of the refugees have slipped back across the border, where they have again been met with force but where the opportunities for hunting have been somewhat better. Meanwhile, reports from far and wide (from the Qu'Appelle Valley west to the foothills) speak of widespread famine—the buffalo are totally gone—and people have been reduced to eating mice, gophers, dogs, horses, even old buffalo hides. People have died, are dying, of starvation.

Yet there's no need for panic, because the Canadian government has everything in hand. With the Pacific Scandal set neatly behind him, Sir John A. Macdonald has returned to the prime minister's office with a new and improved program for national prosperity. No longer content merely with forging a geographical union of provinces linked by steel from coast to coast, Macdonald is now focused on national economic integration. As before, his vision hinges on the settlement of the West. Once the prairies are thickly populated by farmers—including "civilized" Indians—the land will produce such bounty that everyone will be fed, with an abundant surplus left over for sale on world markets. Meanwhile, entrepreneurs in eastern Canada will tool up to meet western demand for farming equipment, building materials, and household goods. Before you know it, the rails will be humming with westbound shipments of plows and cookstoves and outgoing boxcars of golden grain. It is just a matter of getting the necessary arrangements in place.

Over the preceding decade, the government has been working its way down an extensive To Do list. One of the first items to be checked off was establishing a framework for private land ownership. The incoming settlers would naturally expect to hold title to their farms, so that their lands could be bought and sold or passed down to their sons. But for this to be possible—before the longed-for influx of settlers could be persuaded to risk everything on this Last Best West—the whole wide, windswept run of the grasslands would have to be divided into precisely defined, ownable parcels. And so the work began. By 1874, an international team of surveyors had marked the Canada–U.S. boundary from Manitoba west, bisecting the Benton Trail just south of the Cypress Hills, and then continuing clear across to the Rockies, a span of almost nine hundred miles. Soon thereafter, an invisible network of latitude and longitude began to extend north across the open prairie, trapping the subtleties of the land in its impassive grid. Before the end of the decade, crews from the Dominion Land Survey were at work with their chains and theodolites across the Saskatchewan country, assigning a numerical designation to every section and quarter-section. Silently, unobtrusively, the prairie ecosystem was being transformed into supercolossal real-estate development.

"Do you see the Great White-man coming?" an Aboriginal man asked one of the land speculators who, by the mid-1870s, had begun to haunt the West. No, the other responded. "I do," the speaker continued. "And I hear the tramp of the multitude behind him. When he comes you can drop in behind him and take up all the land claims you want, but until then I caution you to put up no stakes in our country."[7]

Therein lay the other big item on the government's agenda: the Indian Question. The challenge on the Canadian prairies was exactly the same as in the U.S.—to get the Indians to forfeit their traditional territories and settle on government-approved plots, where they could be introduced to the arts of farming and "civilization." North of the border, however, force was not an option. Not only did Canada fancy itself above such brutal tactics, it frankly could not afford a war. (The United States was expending around $20 million a year on fighting its Indians, more than the entire budget of the young and impoverished Dominion.) Instead, the Canadian government again opted for the lofty virtues of order and governance. Beginning in 1871, the nation, on behalf of the Great Mother and in response to repeated requests from Aboriginal leaders, entered into a series of agreements with the Aboriginal people of the plains, starting in present-day Manitoba with Treaties 1, 2, and 3, and then proceeding west and northwest and west again to cover off one vast stretch of the country after another.

Treaty 4, for example, which was signed by the Plains Cree and Nakoda in the Qu'Appelle Valley in 1874, encompassed all the lands south of the South Saskatchewan River as far west as—and including—the Cypress Hills, a principality of about 75,000 square miles. Treaty 6, signed two years later, took in an even larger area—more than 120,000 square miles in all—centering on the Saskatchewan River system, across what would one day become central Saskatchewan and Alberta. Finally, Treaty 7, formalized at Blackfoot Crossing in 1877, dealt with a further 50,000 square miles of desirable farming and grazing land, from the Red Deer River south to the border and from the eastern margin of the Cypress Hills west to the Rocky Mountains. Although the nations of the Niitsítapi had hunted and camped in the Cypress Hills for longer than memory, they were formally alienated from this territory by the boundaries of the treaties.

The treaty documents appeared to reflect a meeting of minds between the various indigenous peoples and the Queen but, in fact, they stood at an intersection of conflicting needs. For the government side, the crux of the matter was the clause in which the Aboriginal signatories agreed to "cede, release, surrender and yield up to the Government of the Dominion of Canada, for Her Majesty the Queen, and Her successors forever, all their rights, titles and privileges whatsoever" to the wide prairie land. (To people hearing these words in translation, the concept of "yielding" something to which they had never claimed "title" was just so much gobbledygook, in keeping with the *whereas's* and *hitherto's* of the rest of the document.) What the Native signatories did take away from the discussions, by contrast, were the promises of help with the traumatic transition that was rapidly bearing down on them.

"The Queen knows that you are poor," the government's spokesman had assured the chiefs at the signing of Treaty 4. "The Queen knows that it is hard to find food for yourselves and [your] children; she knows that the winters are cold, and your children are often hungry...

"The Queen always keeps her word," he went on, "always protects her red men. She learned . . . that bad men from the United States had come into her country and had killed some of her red children. What did she say? This must not be, I will send my men [the police] and will not suffer these bad men to hurt my red children, their lives are very precious to me . . ."

Now, "out of her generous heart and liberal hand," the government's Treaty Commissioner affirmed, "she wants to do something for you, so that when the buffalo get scarcer, and they are scarce enough now, you may be able to do something for yourselves . . ."

"I know," the same spokesman continued two years later, at the signing of Treaty 6, "that the sympathy of the Queen, and her assistance, would be with you in any unforeseen circumstances. You must trust to her generosity . . . All I can promise is that you will be treated kindly . . ."[8]

AND SO, we arrive at midsummer 1879. With a decade of preparation behind him—and with alarming rumors of famine echoing around the North-West—Sir John A. Macdonald is anxious to kick his Indian policy into high gear. His immediate goal is to bring the treaty process to fruition by signing up the few remaining holdouts, fulfilling the government's side of the bargain at a manageable cost, and getting the estimated 23,000 Indians on the Canadian plains established on reserves as quickly as possible. To perform this mission, the prime minister has recently recruited the Honourable Member for Yale, British Columbia, a sometime-surveyor, cattleman, land agent, auctioneer, gold miner, trailblazer, and all-around up-and-comer, who just happens to be one of the prime minister's most loyal supporters in the House of Commons. His name is Edgar Dewdney, and for nearly six weeks, he and his muttonchop whiskers have been making their way across the continent by what (in the absence of Macdonald's railroad) is still the only feasible route, traveling first by train from Toronto to Collingwood, then across the Great Lakes by steamer to Duluth, onward by rail to Bismarck, up the Missouri by steamboat to Fort Benton, and thence by horse-drawn wagon to his first official port of call in the Canadian Interior. With a relief that we can only imagine, his team pulls over the final ridge and his destination comes into view: a huddle of whitewashed buildings surrounded by a rustic stockade, flanked by a straggling town site, and embraced by a circle of hills. Welcome to Fort Walsh, Mr. Indian Commissioner.

As it happens, Ned Dewdney is not the only high muck-a-muck who is in residence at the fort. In fact, he has traveled cross-country with the top officers of the North-West Mounted Police—Commissioner James Macleod and his wife, Mary, and Assistant Commissioner Irvine—together with a fresh intake of horses and eighty-one new men, recruited in the East as police reinforcements. Almost the only notable who won't be here is the fort's commanding office, Inspector Walsh, who is focusing his time and attention on the Lakota camp at Wood Mountain. Evicting a few dozen whiskey traders had been nothing compared with the challenge of getting a few thousand unwanted Indians across the border. With the Sioux now at the forefront, Fort Walsh has recently been upgraded to serve as Mountie headquarters, with an official residence for the commissioner, barracks for a garrison of up to 150 men, and an armory of seven-pound field guns, or small cannons.

Celebrating their first Christmas in their roomy new mess hall, the men of "B" Division had sat down to dinner beneath a portrait of their absent commanding officer, his handsome visage framed in greenery and bracketed by a festive display of six-shooters, carbines, and lances. Under the picture, ingeniously worked with curb chains and bits against a background of black cloth, someone had outlined the triumphant words "Sitting Bull's Boss."

On the subject of the "American hostiles," Commissioner Dewdney's instructions are clear. He is to keep Ottawa informed of their whereabouts and do whatever he can to hurry them back across the border. Under no circumstances is he to authorize an issue of rations. "Sitting Bull and his people, seeing that the buffalo is failing them in our territory, will go back to their own country," Ottawa has decreed, "the only other alternative being starvation for themselves, their wives, and their families."[9] But this hard line obviously cannot be taken with Canada's "own" Indians, at least not with those who, by taking treaty, have recently accepted the hand of the Queen in friendship.

Although Dewdney is not a greenhorn—fifteen years in British Columbia had put paid to that—he knows nothing about the prairie or the buffalo or the people who depend on them. (When he'd pointed this deficiency out to Macdonald, his boss had been unmoved. "Indians are all alike," the prime minister had assured him.[10]) Yet despite his ignorance of local conditions, Dewdney knows trouble when it stares him in the face. "Continually meeting hungry Indians," he'd noted in his journal on the way up from Fort Benton. "Saw a few [pronghorn] antelope, but no buffalo," he'd scribbled the following day. "Lots of old dried carcasses all over the prairie."[11] So he isn't surprised to find a large number of gaunt-looking Indians congregated at the fort, waiting for him and Macleod to put in an appearance. And he is gratified two days later when a delegation of Nakoda men ride up in procession, looking "very pretty" with their treaty flag flying overhead, and acknowledge his importance with a display of precision horsemanship.

Like many an immigrant before and since, Indian Commissioner Dewdney is a man on the make. (A child of the English tenements who has somehow managed to pass as upper class, he will die a wealthy man, enriched by kickbacks on government contracts and insider land transactions.) For the moment, his fortunes depend entirely on implementing Macdonald's Indian policy and making it a success, and he doesn't waste any time in getting down to business. All the Aboriginal leaders who have gathered, including Siksika "visitors" from Treaty 7 and Crees and Nakoda from Treaty 4, are called together to confer with Colonel Macleod and the new government chief.

The Siksika, Crees, and Nakoda have come to the fort with an urgent agenda to press. In the short term, they desperately need supplies to sustain them until they can reach the main herds of buffalo, now south of the Milk River and under assault by all the subsistence and market hunters on the continent. In the longer term, they entreat the government to fulfill its promise (made explicitly in Treaty 6 and implicitly in all the rest) to provide emergency assistance in times of famine. In reply, Colonel Macleod speaks of the government's "great sorrow" at their suffering but reminds them that they must not expect assistance every time their stomachs growl. There is a difference between mere hunger, he informs them, and starvation. In the long run, the government expects them to "work and earn their own living,"[12] and that is why Mr. Dewdney has been sent to concern himself exclusively with their interests. He has come, Macleod tells the Indians, to show you how to live.

When the conference reconvenes the following day, "Whitebeard," as the delegation quickly nicknames Dewdney, outlines the details of the government's plan. He explains that he has brought two farmers with him from the East, with others to follow soon, and that they will immediately set to work breaking the soil and raising crops for seed and food. In addition, he tells his attentive audience, the government will send instructors to show you how to farm, so you can work the soil the same as the white man does. If only you will settle down, in two or three years—it's a promise— you will be independent and have plenty to live on, without any need for handouts from the government.

There are nods all around at this prospect, and two of the leading chiefs—Cuwiknak eyaku (The Man Who Took the Coat) for the Nakoda and Ka-wezauce (Cowessess or Little Child) for his mixed community of Saulteaux and Cree—rise to express their assent. They are eager to choose their reserves as soon as possible, somewhere in their home country of the Cypress Hills, and settle to the task of becoming farmers. But meanwhile, what they all need are rations to take them south to the herds. "Gave them some Beef & Flour," Whitebeard notes in his journal after the meeting has adjourned. "They are awful beggars, but I think they are really hungry." [13]

No sooner has this business been settled than another large group of people arrives at the fort. Here is another opportunity for Dewdney to turn on his voluble charm and advance the government's ambitions. The newcomers are non-treaty people, followers of the Plains Cree leaders Minahikosis, or Little Pine, and Mistahi-maskwa, known in English as Big Bear. More discussions are convened, and Dewdney repeats his pitch: Choose your reserves, take advantage of the government's generous assistance as you learn how to farm, and your future will be secure. Two days later, on July 2, 1879, Little Pine, with his 324 followers, enters the fort to sign an adhesion to Treaty 6. With him—taking advantage of Dewdney's new edict that any leader with a hundred followers can take treaty as a chief—is a headman from Big Bear's band, Papewes, or Lucky Man. It is not easy to resist a hand held out in generosity when your children are starving.

"Gave some Beef, Tobacco, Tea & Sugar to those who took the Treaty," Dewdney notes in his diary that night. "Big Bear would like to come in but he is afraid of being laughed at." [14]

Yet even in the face of Dewdney's derision, even as rations are handed out to their friends, Big Bear and his remaining supporters hold strong in their dissenting position.

"We want none of the Queen's presents," Mistahi-maskwa had once told a government official. "When we set a fox-trap, we scatter pieces of meat all around. But when the fox gets into the trap, we knock him on the head."[15] Always dubious about the adequacy of the treaties and the government's sincerity in entering into them, Big Bear remains polite but steadfast in his discussions with Whitebeard.

"He wanted more land and more money," Dewdney reports to his masters in Ottawa, after the two have met. "He said he wanted to see how [the treaties] worked with the other Indians."[16]

Still, even if Big Bear hasn't been brought onside, Dewdney has to admit to a grudging admiration for him. "I have not formed such a poor opinion of 'Big Bear,' " he confesses, "as some appear to have done. He is of a very independent character, self-reliant and appears to know how to make his own living without begging from the Government."[17] All in all, the Indian Commissioner's ten-day visit to Fort Walsh has been time well spent. As he clambers back into his buckboard to continue his tour of the West, he is confident that the government's new Indian policy will prove a splendid success.

From our vantage point on the hillside, we watch as the Indian Commissioner rattles over the western rim of the valley and disappears from sight. The sun is low; there's a chill in the air. It's going to be a long night.

{NINE}

THE HUNGER CAMP

*Our people realized they had lost their land
and they scattered all over like little birds.*
ISABELLE LITTLE BEAR, granddaughter of Big Bear,
in 1958, recalling the early 1880s

A COMMEMORATIVE SITE like Fort Walsh inevitably has its ghosts, who may be either remembered with pride or prudently kept in the dark, their memory buried in archives or the dust of old books. But an ordinary place is different, and no place on earth could be more ordinary than the puddle on the prairie known as Cypress Lake. Located partway between Fort Walsh and Eastend, it's an oversized slough that has been "enhanced" by a dam, giving it the bloated outline and mucky, crusted shore of a water impoundment. Hydrologically speaking, the lake is more interesting than it at first appears, since it not only stores spring floodwaters from Battle Creek but also serves as the source of the Frenchman River. All the same, it's hard to believe that anything of importance could ever have happened here.

If you happen to be in the vicinity, the lake is easy enough to find. It can be reached from either Fort Walsh or Eastend via pavement that gives way to gravel and then dwindles to a rough track before debouching at the optimistically named Cypress Lake Provincial Recreation Site. But if people actually come here to recreate, they clearly don't come in droves. The site is equipped with an uneven rank of picnic tables (sans picnickers) set under drought-stressed trees, a serviceable wharf and boat dock (sans boaters), and—as an unexpected touch of cheer—a couple of pots of petunias tagged with a wistful request for anyone who happens by to please water them.

The atmosphere is thick with silence, and when you move, you seem to leave ripples in your wake. You might be swimming through quicksilver. And this unearthly mood is not quite broken by the delight of watching butcher birds—rare loggerhead shrikes—plunging from the trees to the ground to catch grasshoppers, which they then stuff, one by one, into the beaks of their insatiable young. The heaviness doesn't even lift entirely when you gaze across the lake and discover that the bright dots along the far shore, viewed through binoculars, are actually a flotilla of white pelicans, huge and dazzling in the glimmer. Everything that is here carries an echo of something that is not. Trapped between lake and sky, this is a world that has been hollowed out.

THAT SAME description could be applied to an old photo I came across one day, on the website of the Canadian national archives in Ottawa. In a sense, it's a picture of nothing, the same kind of emptiness that you find at Cypress Lake. It might even have been taken there, and I used to think that it was, though after examining it more closely I'm not so certain. In the photo, a featureless sky hangs over a featureless prairie landscape inset with a featureless pond that bleeds out of the picture frame along the right margin. In the foreground, two horses are drinking, hock deep in the water, while nearby, along the shore, two child-sized figures are seated in identical slumped postures. Their faces are turned away from the camera and from one another as well, and each figure appears to be lost in its own small world. Across the center of the image, a scattered line of conical tipis, some distinct, others smudged by distance, extends along the horizon, spanning a low run of hills. By my count, there are more than sixty dwellings in the encampment, with shelter for several hundred souls. How odd that except for the huddled figures in the foreground, no one else is in view. And how disconcerting that some kind of corrosion has set in around the edges of the picture and appears to be creeping toward the center, like an incursion of fungus.

According to the archival records, this photograph shows "Big Bear's (Cree) Camp, Maple Creek, Saskatchewan" on June 6, 1883, as it was seen through the lens of one George M. Dawson of the Geological Survey of Canada. Just as a matter of interest, it is worth noting that Dawson also deserves credit as the first scientist to discover dinosaur bones in southwestern Saskatchewan and as one of the first to appreciate the stratigraphic importance of the Cypress Hills. In the summer of 1883, however, he was merely passing through, bound from Ottawa via Fort Benton to the Crow's Nest Pass, on a mission to survey that region's massive coal deposits. (Settlement could not proceed without a railroad; trains could not run without fuel; it was all part of Macdonald's transcontinental megaproject.) But it's a shame Dawson was in such a hurry that summer that he didn't have time to stop. If he'd ridden into the Cree camp and asked for a cup of tea, he would have encountered the nightmare side of the national dream. Sit back and light your pipe: it's quite the story.

IT IS summer 1883. Four years have elapsed since White-beard made his first tour of the Canadian North-West, dispensing gifts and promises. Life had been hard before he arrived, and it has been worse ever since. That first fall, 1879, the Métis at Chimney Coulee had enjoyed a reasonable harvest, filling their carts with buffalo hides and pemmican for transport to Fort Qu'Appelle, but it would never happen again. By early winter, grass fires had broken out all along the border, keeping the buffalo south of the line. Some people, including the Canadian authorities, said that the fires had been set by American soldiers under orders to starve out the Lakota "hostiles," who were still holed up at East End and Wood Mountain. Others pointed a finger at the commercial hide hunters or at the Aboriginal people themselves, whether "British" or American. Worst of all was the possibility that the fires had been an act of nature, or an act of the gods, and that the buffalo people had been forsaken by the powers who had sustained their ancestors.

Then, as if to compound the misery, the weather turned brutally cold. With the backing of the Canadian government, hundreds of people—including Métis families from Chimney Coulee and Cree bands led by Big Bear, Little Pine, and Lucky Man, among others—fled south to the Milk River in Montana to search for buffalo. As many as five thousand other half-starved people huddled at Fort Walsh and in tattered camps around the Cypress Hills, hoping against hope that the Great Mother would keep her word. And so, for a time, she did, sending her red-coated policemen into the cold and storms with rations of flour and beef. When spring finally came, the Queen continued to keep her commitments by doing what she could to help her "red children" make the transition from hunting to agriculture. As soon as the frost was out of the ground, the two farmers who had arrived with Dewdney set to work breaking the land and, with the assistance of Native crews, seeding small fields of grain and vegetables.

Soon, everything was clicking along exactly as Whitebeard had said. When The Man Who Took the Coat requested a reserve for the Nakoda at the westernmost end of the hills, from the summit all the way down onto the plains to the north, his proposal was accepted at once. Within months, an official survey had been completed, and the documents were sent off to Ottawa for an approving rubber stamp. Meanwhile, Cowessess and his people (one of the other bands who had taken treaty during Dewdney's initial visit) selected land along Maple Creek, north and east of the fort, although in their case, the survey had to be postponed. All over the country, bands were eager to select their lands and start producing crops, and the government surveyor simply could not be everywhere at once. His services were urgently required in the Qu'Appelle Valley and along the North Saskatchewan, where numerous signatories of Treaties 4 and 6 had elected to settle down.

But no need to worry: everything in due course. As soon as the surveyor was freed up, he'd be back not only to look after Cowessess but also to establish reserves for several other leaders—notably the new Treaty 6 chiefs Little Pine and Lucky Man, together with two chiefs from Treaty 4, Piapot (Payepot), or Hole-in-the-Sioux, and Nekaneet, or Foremost Man—all of whom had requested land in the Cypress Hills. Too bad about the delays. Simply unavoidable.

New country, blah, blah, blah. But rest assured that, given time, all the t's would be crossed and i's dotted, and everything would be arranged.

Meanwhile, on the height of land at the Nakoda reserve, wheat was pushing out of the ground for the first time in history, and the carefully hilled fields of potatoes looked green and promising. For a crazy, fleeting moment, it was almost possible to believe that Dewdney had told the truth and that things would be coming up roses before you knew it.

Disaster struck in late summer, in the form of a killing frost—not entirely exceptional at an altitude of four thousand feet—and Dewdney's too-easy promises were blighted in a single night. The grain had to be cut for green feed; the potatoes turned to slime in the bin. Although the red coats continued to provide rations, there was never enough to eat. Thus began the terrible winter of 1880–81, when the Nakoda were forced to kill and eat their precious horses to keep from starving.

But even in the face of this setback, the Canadian government kept up its front of good cheer. Quoth Sir John A. Macdonald in his wrap-up report for 1881, "The condition of Indian Affairs in the Territories has, on the whole, been satisfactory during the past year."[1] In private, however, he and his officials had begun to acknowledge the unpalatable truth: the entire North-West was in crisis. Although ragged groups of buffalo were still occasionally found north of the border, they were walking dead, too few and too far between to sustain even themselves. The only significant herds, while they lasted, were in Montana, around the Missouri and the Milk, mostly on the large but soon-to-be-diminished Indian reservation that flanked the American side of the border. In theory, the Canadian government had obtained emergency permission for "British" Indians and

Métis to cross the line and hunt, a concession that, by Dewdney's estimate, had already saved eastern taxpayers 100,000 bucks. (Bands who were out hunting didn't have to be rationed.) In practice, however, Montanans were aghast at Washington's largess and gave the intruders a surly welcome.

Hundreds of blue-coated soldiers—now garrisoned at a massive brick stronghold called Fort Assinniboine, just across the line—kept the intruders under close watch, ready to pounce at the first hint of possible trouble. One day, for instance, members of a hunting party from Big Bear's camp on the Milk River were butchering sixty buffalo that they'd had the good fortune to kill when a troop of American cavalry, armed with cannons, descended on them, confiscated their horses, and ordered them back to camp. When two of the hunters protested, the soldiers beat them up and left them injured on the ground.

Back in the Cree village, Big Bear and his councilors decided that rather than attempt to retaliate—"Our strength is nothing . . . we are strangers here"—they would send their head chief to Fort Assinniboine on a peace mission. Here is how the meeting went, as recalled in detail by an eyewitness.[2]

"In peace I come and would speak," Big Bear told the fort's commander, through an interpreter.

"Yes, I'm listening," the tall, thin officer replied curtly.

"I have done no wrong," Big Bear said. "My people get blamed for everything that happens but we have done nothing. We have come to this land to make our livelihood, to support ourselves."

"Yes?"

"I come to you today with a good heart, thinking that you will have a touch of sympathy for us, that you will pity us. We are poor and in a bad way. I have come to ask you to give us back our horses."

The officer did not have to search for an answer. "Obviously you do not understand our laws here," he retorted. "Plenty of cattle are missing in our country, and we blame you people from Canada . . . If I carried out my orders to the letter of the law, I would take everything you have, not just your horses, but your guns, your lodges, and your clothes, until you would have nothing left."

"But we have little or nothing now," Big Bear objected.

"You are thieves from another land," the officer shouted, "and you should be shot like dogs! If you had behaved yourselves in the first place you would have been treated well and this wouldn't have happened. You will not get your horses back."

Here at least was a point on which Big Bear and the Canadian government might have agreed: The Great Father was armed and ornery.

NORTH OF the border, the milk of human kindness was drying up as well, not that it had ever been very abundant. Faced with a choice between the barren teat of the Great Mother and the armed embrace of the United States, the Lakota refugees had been brought to the breaking point. As the months of exile crept by with no action, it had become apparent that the Macdonald government meant exactly what it had said and that Canada was prepared to stand by and watch the refugees starve to death. This conclusion was reinforced, in the summer of 1880, when Inspector Walsh was suddenly taken off the case—"Sitting Bull's Boss" no more—and a hard-line officer was sent in as his replacement. (Walsh had drawn the ire of his superiors by trying to be the hero, getting chummy with Sitting Bull, and generally playing both ends against the middle.)

A few months later, Chief Spotted Eagle and his followers left their camp near the East End police post and headed
across the line, where they surrendered their guns, their
horses, and their freedom. Sitting Bull held on for one final
winter, but by July of 1881, he too had given up, and he and
his people turned themselves over to American authorities
at Fort Buford. A number of families chose to remain at Wood
Mountain, still hoping for a reserve, and their request would
be granted, in a token way, after a wait of forty-nine years.

If the Lakota refugees were on their way down and out,
Canada's treaty Indians were supposed to be on their way up,
on a fast track toward prosperity and independence. Yet, in
the spring of 1881, when Indian Affairs had sent a chief from
the Qu'Appelle Valley to Fort Walsh on a mission to persuade people who were receiving rations there to head east
and settle on their reserves, things had not gone as planned.
Instead of staying on message, the chief had spoken urgently
about sickness and hunger in the Qu'Appelle and told everyone to stay where they were. The tension had continued to
intensify throughout the summer, as twelve hundred people from the Saskatchewan River country deserted their
reserves and fled to the Cypress Hills. The nights throbbed
with drum songs, and the atmosphere crackled with bitter
stories about shoddy farm equipment, wild oxen, stringy
cattle, incompetent instructors, inedible rations—hunger,
always hunger—and the blatant inadequacy of the treaties.

The official response was unsympathetic. Yes, there
may have been a few glitches, the authorities admitted, but that was no excuse for getting all riled up. Just go
home, get back to work, and stop "exciting sedition."[3] Indians were such awful complainers; you just couldn't satisfy
them. Meanwhile, emergency updates and instructions

were crisscrossing the continent in frantic telegrams—
Fort Walsh to Dewdney in Winnipeg, Winnipeg to head
office, Ottawa to Winnipeg to Fort Walsh—their meaning
carefully enshrouded in a secret code. In the absence of an all-
Canadian telegraph system, the messages had to be sent by
mail to Fort Assinniboine and east via the United States. If
the Americans found out what was happening or, worse yet,
if the Canadian newspapers were to catch on, there would
be no end of hell to pay in Ottawa. Better to keep the trouble
hush-hush.

> *Telegram, Dewdney to Ottawa, July 16, 1881* [report-
> ing from Fort Walsh]: abridge suspicious decayed
> Jeweler incommoded propitiously Moral Persuasion
> about explaining Incommoded relax transaction inert-
> ness Granulate nutmeg fornication resumes redeemable
> overturned abrogating Walsh amulet fornication
> abridged Fergus ottoman unconscionable transaction
> Inertness zenith be left there to their own resources
> thwarting articulately nowadays Shears transaction
> surgery from our pursuing such a course[4]

> *Translation, scribbled in pencil, between the lines* [report-
> ing from Fort Walsh]: A sumptuous dance is in progress.
> Moral Persuasion about exhausted in regards to Indians
> going north for reservations. Recommend our aban-
> doning Walsh altogether for a year or two. The Indians
> would be left there to their own resources. There are no
> settlers to suffer from our pursuing such a course.

In the government's codebook, "Inertness" stood for
"Indians," to be pruned back by "settlers," or "Shears." An

"unconscionable transaction" remained as unconscionable
as ever.

THE TENSION that had been simmering all summer came
to a boil that August 1881. By then, there were about 3,300
treaty people congregated in the hills, against a garrison
at Fort Walsh of 97 police. The balance tipped even further
when Chiefs Little Pine and Lucky Man, with all their followers, came in from the south to receive their annual treaty
payments. (The treaties provided for a yearly dispersal of $5
per person, $15 for a councilor, and $25 for a chief, as a reaf-
firmation of goodwill and the terms for a lasting peace.) As
members of the Cree camps in Montana, the newcomers
had spent most of the previous two years struggling to support themselves. Now, they joined the struggle to hold the
Canadian authorities accountable for their errors and omis-
sions. My people and I will not accept our payments, Little
Pine declared, unless our relatives whom the government
describes as "half-breeds" are added to the treaty lists and
allowed to share in the meager benefits.

The officials at the fort dismissed this idea out of hand,
arguing that the Métis had been dealt with back in the
1870s when, after the Riel Rebellion, each adult male had
been granted either a half-section of land or an equivalent
in "half-breed scrip." Not so, Chief Little Pine said. These
people in the hills had never been given land, and anyone
could see that they were in a bad way now. Admit them to
the treaties, Little Pine said, or—

WELL AWARE of their precarious position, the police wasted
no time in responding to the unspoken threat. A fatigue was
immediately ordered to clear out the bastions (which had

been used for storing oats) and to build emplacements for the four seven-pound cannons. A field gun soon stared vacantly in each direction, armed and dangerous. Meanwhile, the constables were issued with extra Winchesters and confined to the fort, ready for action at a moment's notice.

And then the whole protest fizzled even faster than it had blown up. If there is a force stronger than the call of justice, it is the call of clothing, shelter, and food. Buffalo had been sighted just east of the hills. *Otapanihowin:* Livelihood. In their relief, the hunters set aside their grievances, collected their treaty payments, and prepared to set out for the plains. Drums pounded in jubilation and brightly dressed riders galloped around the parade ground, performing precision maneuvers, swinging under their horses' necks as if, for the moment, life was worth celebrating again. But the Canadian government was in no mood for partying.

By the end of the summer, the Great Mother had snapped. As embodied by bureaucrats like Edgar Dewdney, she was officially fed up with trying to keep control of the "large numbers of Worthless and lazy Indians" who had been drawn to the Cypress Hills.[5] If only the Indians had done as they were told, Dewdney argued, if they had stayed on their reserves and put in an honest day's work, they would not now be in such a fractious and perilous condition. As for suggestions that the government might be partly to blame for the failure of its Indian policies—well, honestly, such statements hardly deserved a response. Let me tell you, the bureaucrats blustered, what the real problem is: Indians are too primitive and childlike to know what is good for them. It is time for a firm hand to take over, in loco parentis.

What the situation demanded, Dewdney decided, was a complete clear-out of the Cypress Hills. Fort Walsh would be closed at the earliest possible juncture, not just for a year or two but permanently. The farm on Maple Creek would be abandoned—too bad, since it alone of the government's efforts had proven a success—and past commitments regarding reserves in the hills were hereby suspended. From now on, all efforts were to focus on "persuading" the Indians to accept reserves in the Battleford district or the Qu'Appelle, in accordance with the government's sense of their tribal affiliations and homelands. To encourage compliance, rations would be withheld from anyone who lingered, except in the most dire of circumstances, when agents were allowed to provide just enough aid to keep people from starving to death. If anyone suffered under these directives, it would be their own fault. "The longer they continue to act against the wishes of the Government," Dewdney wrote, "the more wretched will they become."[6]

These orders were in violation of the oral and written texts of the treaties, which had promised freedom of movement, an equal say in reserve selection, and kindness in times of urgent need. But what did those flowery old promises matter when Macdonald's railway was finally a-building and the long-anticipated inrush of settlers was about to be unleashed. The Indians had to be brought into line, whatever the means.

It was under this draconian rule that a hunger camp began to assemble on the shores of Cypress Lake. Piapot and his people were among the first to arrive, in December of 1881, in the twilight of *pawacakinasisi-pisîm*, the Blizzard Moon. Fortunately, fish could be drawn up from under the ice, and pathetic clusters of bachelor bulls still sometimes wandered by, providing the camp with the means to survive. Every couple of weeks, someone would walk to Fort Walsh and ask for a handful of cartridges, a few fish hooks, or a small ration of flour. "The Indians are certainly doing their best to hunt and gain their own living," the Indian agent observed.[7] Still, when he tried to get them to do chores around the fort in return for his assistance (since it was universally agreed that charity without a return of work would cause irreparable moral harm), he noticed that they were sometimes reluctant to comply. "As a great many had no moccasins and all were poorly clad, it was difficult to get them to go out in the cold," he reported.[8]

When spring came, the camp at the lake was enlarged by several hundred additional souls, as the people who had been hunting in Montana again began fleeing north. The American military, tired of playing its lethal game of cat-and-mouse with the "British" intruders, had finally resorted to a full-out assault to get rid of the "foreigners." Little Pine and Lucky Man arrived at the lake in early April—*ayik-pisîm*, the Frog Moon—to the dismaying news that they were also being evicted from the Cypress Hills. To compound the injury, the Great Mother, with whom the two returning chiefs had smoked the pipe in treaty less than three years before, was now threatening to starve them into obeying her orders.

By the time Big Bear came into camp a few weeks later, the program of removals was already well advanced. Cowessess and The Man Who Took the Coat were among the first to leave, though both were "very loath to go."[9] Piapot and his people followed in midsummer. Their six-week journey east to the Qu'Appelle was marred by unfit rations, sickness, and several deaths. One old man was so distressed by the death of his granddaughter that he killed himself en route by thrusting a sharp stick down his esophagus.

At Cypress Lake, meanwhile, the last holdouts from the government's plans were getting by as best they could. A collective appeal to the fort for help accomplished nothing—the police just rolled out their cannons again—and tangling with the American forces was now out of the question. Perhaps the best option would be to bow to the Great Mother's wishes, as the other leaders had done. Weeks dragged into months without easy answers, and the children became so exhausted by hunger that they could no longer even cry. Surely, life on one of the government's reserves could not be worse than this misery. Then, in *kaskatinow-pisîm,* the Freezing-up Moon of October, Piapot and The Man Who Took the Coat, with their people, straggled back into camp with stories of their horrific experience in the Qu'Appelle, where the ground was littered with the bones of people who had died of smallpox years before. The government had sent them to a place called the Skull Mountainettes to sicken and starve in the land of the dead.

What they wanted, the returnees told the authorities, was what they had always wanted and what had once been promised to them. They wanted to select their reserves and settle in the Cypress Hills. Speaking for the Nakoda, The Man Who Took the Coat explained that he and his people had been brought up in this country and that, for them, the land was filled with stories and ceremony. It held them close to their ancestors, including the relatives and friends who had been lost to the white man's anger ten years earlier. This was the first time he had refused to do what the Queen wanted, the chief said, but he loved the hills and hoped that the government would not be angry with him. The officers at the fort nodded as if they understood, but they insisted that the government knew best. The people would have to leave the hills or face the consequences.

AS ANOTHER winter closed in, two officials from the North-West Mounted Police—a visiting bureaucrat named

Frederick White and the police physician, Dr. Augustus
Jukes—were sent out to assess conditions in the Indian
camps. White was an old hand in the civil service, with
an insider's knowledge of government ways and means.
Although he recognized human extremity when he saw
it—"a more wretched half starved camp could not be imagined," he wrote—he also knew that Mr. Dewdney would
receive this news with a measure of satisfaction.[10]

"Of course they have asked again to have reservations here," White reported, "and say they may as well
starve to death here as on the reservations North and East,
but... limited rations, absence of game, scarcity of clothing, and the suffering they must endure this winter...will I
hope bring them to their senses by next spring."

Dr. Jukes, by contrast, was stricken by what he observed.
"There are now encamped in the immediate vicinity of Fort
Walsh, about two thousand Indians," he informed his superiors, all "literally in a starving condition and destitute of
the commonest necessaries of life.

"The disappearance of the Buffalo," he continued, "has
left them not only without food but also without Robes,
mocassins and adequate Tents or 'Teppees' to shield them
from the inclemency of the impending winter. Few of their
lodges are of Buffalo hide, the majority being of cotton only,
many of these in the most rotten and dilapidated condition,
a few consisting only of branches laid upon the lodge poles,
a terribly insufficient protection against the wind, frost and
snow of the severe winter of this exposed region.

"The absence of... an adequate number of lodges to
cover so large a number has rendered great overcrowding
of these wretched tenements necessary and in all visited by
me today the extreme scarcity of robes, blankets or indeed
of any other covering for the wretched inmates at night was

painfully apparent. Their clothing for the most part was miserable and scanty in the extreme. I saw little children at this inclement season, snow having already fallen, who had scarcely rags to cover them. Of food they possessed little or none." (The daily ration had fallen to four ounces of flour and two ounces of dried meat, per person, and was grudgingly dispensed.)

"It would indeed be difficult to exaggerate their extreme wretchedness and need or the urgent necessity which exists for some prompt and sufficient provision being made for them by the Government . . . I have no hesitation in declaring my belief that unless speedy and adequate measures are taken to provide these suffering people with the common necessaries of life the result will be disastrous and even appalling." [11]

Wretched. Disastrous. Appalling. Surely those were words to make a person reflect on the frailty of human life. But not the new lieutenant-governor, the Honourable Mr. Dewdney, who pooh-poohed the reports. "It must be recollected," he advised the prime minister, "that Dr. Jukes has not had much experience with Indians." [12] To the officer in charge at Fort Walsh, he wrote: "I hope you will impress upon the Indians that they have brought their present helpless condition on themselves." His sole concession, assented to "with great reluctance," was to authorize the payment of the annuities that were due to Little Pine, Lucky Man, Piapot, and the other treaty chiefs, so that they might purchase blankets and clothing. [13] Big Bear and his people, as non-treaty, would continue to receive nothing.

As the winter deepened and another Blizzard Moon drew near, the agent at Fort Walsh sent an update to his boss. "The Indians look very bad," he told Dewdney. "I know they are not getting enough flour but I like to punish them a little. I will have to increase their rations, but not much."[14] No need for a cipher to keep this news under wraps: the cold heart of the Canadian government was no secret.

A few weeks later, on December 8, 1882, Big Bear entered Fort Walsh and, concerned as ever to do his best for his followers, signed an adhesion to Treaty 6. When the snow lifted the following spring, all the people who had wintered in the hills packed up their pitiful belongings and set out, under armed escort, to their appointed reserves. Piapot and The Man Who Took the Coat were sent back to the Qu'Appelle Valley. Little Pine, Lucky Man, and Big Bear were instructed to go north. By *opaskowi-pisîm*, July, when the ducks were molting and flightless, the people had been dispersed, and the land around Cypress Lake lay empty and silent.

TEN

CREATION STORIES

There really is no such thing as empty space.
CURLY BEAR WAGNER, Cody, WY, 2000

THE SMALL, dark-haired woman on the other side of the table looks up from her beadwork and sees the ripple of pain that tracks across my face. "It's not you," she says consolingly, misreading my distress. "It's not you that got treated bad that time. It was them people, back then."

Her name is Piyêso kâ-pêtowitak, Thunder Coming Sounds Good, also known as Jean Francis Oakes, and we are sitting in her bright, comfortable kitchen on a summit of the Cypress Hills, northeast of Eastend, southwest of Maple Creek, and about half an hour, as the crow flies, from whatever remains of the hunger camp at Cypress Lake. There must still be traces of that unhappy site—grave mounds or circles of stone—but I have never been able to convince myself to search them out. There are limits to my capacity for shame and sadness.

Shame? I wasn't the one who had withheld food from starving people to force them to submit. It wasn't me who pledged a friendship that was supposed to last forever—"so long as the rivers would flow, so long as the grass shall grow"—and almost immediately went back on my word.[1] I'd never slaughtered a buffalo or shot a grizzly or poisoned a single wolf. My grandpa was only a glint in his father's eye when it had all happened. Yet no matter how I rail and squirm against the sins of the past, one unerodible truth still stands. As the descendant of incomers to the Canadian prairies, I am the intended beneficiary, however unwittingly, of an ecological and humanitarian atrocity.

No wonder settler-historians, including even bright sparks like Wallace Stegner, have insisted on an emphatic division between the Old West and the New, between the crude brutality of the frontier and the perceived civility of the modern world. If Old and New are defined as distinctly separate strata, then scholars can assign the meanness of Western history to a distant and semimythical past that seems to have no connection to the present. But sadly for our peace of mind, that's not the way things happened. Instead, as the Cypress Hills have been at some pains to teach me, the New West of our daily lives lies comfortably, if uncomfortably, on a foundation of abuse and loss.

The grand narrative of prairie settlement is not just a collection of up-by-the-bootstraps stories told by people like Marie Nibus (who described her life in the Eastend history book), gallantly scrubbing the floorboards of a two-room tarpaper shack or driving a horse and buggy across the mural in Jack's Café. Even opening up the frame to admit failure, as embodied by people like Stegner's tumbleweed of a dad, doesn't tell the whole truth. To really acknowledge what happened, we also have to write in the tens of thousands of displaced people, refugees in their home and native lands, who were launched on a journey of desolation.

I had always known this, albeit hazily, in a through-a-glass-darkly kind of way. The trouble had lurked, like a disquieting shadow, around the edges of my upbringing. Why weren't there any Indians on the Indian Quarter, where my family went to swim in the dark, spruce-green waters of the Beaverlodge River? Why were the two women of my imaginings unable to move or raise a hand in greeting? Now here I was, decades later and hundreds of miles distant, face-to-face with the same old loneliness and isolation. Enough of this, I thought. Enough already.

And meanwhile, there was still that strange sensation, now stronger than ever before, that Keith and I had tripped over these hills for a reason. Something I couldn't name seemed to be urging me on, challenging me to pay attention and remember. The imperative seemed to emanate from the hills themselves, with their treasury of bones and stones and narratives. Something in me had decided to honor this land and its stories as best I could, and to do so, I was going to need help. It was time to get a move on and start making some new connections.

Interview with the late Chief Nekaneet, home office, Savage-Bell residence, Saskatoon, SK, April 4, 2011, 11:33 AM

C.S.: In English, they called you Front Man or Foremost Man, is that correct?

CHIEF N.: I am the one who walks ahead, *kani'kanit*, the leader. You can call me Nekaneet.

C.S.: I've read that you were born in the Cypress Hills.

CHIEF N.: Yes, I have been born and raised in this part of the country, and I came back here when it was my time to die. That was in the springtime, 1897.[2]

C.S.: You came back here from Montana?

CHIEF N.: Yes, we went all over those days—Medicine Hat, Maple Creek, Swift Current. We hunted, we gathered up the buffalo bones from the prairie and sold them so we could eat. We polished the buffaloes' horns and took them to the station to sell when the train stopped and people got off. We worked for white men on ranches, haying, making fences. Canada, Montana, too. All over our old lands, where we used to hunt for buffalo and go to trade before.

One time, it was in *yiyîkopîwi-pîsim*, the Frost Moon, November [1881]. We were at Cypress Lake that time, and the buffalo were gone. The white men at Fort Walsh wouldn't feed us, and eight of us, we went to Fort Belknap in Montana to trade. We thought it would be good there. They said Piapot, my uncle, had paid the chief at Assinniboine to let us come. But the blue-coated soldiers took us to their brick house and put us in a dark room. They kept our guns, our knives, even some of our clothes, and then they took us to the boundary line. The weather was cold already. We had no horses, nothing, not even moccasins. They gave us food for one night and told us to walk to the camp at Cypress Lake. Two of our men died on the way, and we had to leave them lying and carry them in afterwards.

[He pauses and looks down at his hands. Folds and unfolds them. Takes a deep breath and goes on.]

After that, the white men at Fort Walsh said they would feed us if we went to the reserve at Qu'Appelle. But we knew they did not like to keep their promises.

C.S.: You did go to the Qu'Appelle, though, didn't you? Because you didn't have any choice?

CHIEF N.: [nods] Colonel Irvine, the big chief of the police, he came here with a government man, that Wadsworth.[3] He said we could choose the best land for a reserve, here in the Cypress Hills. Piapot was there that time, and so was I and all the head men. We chose the valley [twelve miles south of the town of Maple Creek] because the grass was good, and there was not much snow or cold weather. Our horses could feed all winter on the prairie, and we could grow potatoes and grain and live like our white brothers. Colonel Irvine said the Great Mother had given this land to us and marked it with a pile of stones. It was to be for us and our children.

Three moons after, that Wadsworth told us we had to go to the reserve at Qu'Appelle where the snow was deep. The next summer, they took us down in wagons. But when we got there, there were no plows or hoes, and we came back here. That was another winter, 1882, when we stopped at Cypress Lake.[4]

The next spring, they sent The Man Who Took the Coat and the Assiniboines down to the Qu'Appelle again on the iron road, and they made that wagon run off its rails. They tried to kill them all. But the Great Spirit watched over the children, and nobody was killed. Piapot was given a wagon and horses, because he was our chief, and we went with our horses. But still there were no plows on that reserve and not enough food. Forty-two of our people died [out of 550].[5] So my people and I came back to the hills in 1884, because this is a good country here.

C.S.: But you had no land. There was nothing for you here.

CHIEF N.: [squares his shoulders, raises his chin] We made our own survival. That time, we had one spade to plant our potatoes, and we dug the ground with axes. The government had forgotten the reserve it had promised to us. I wrote to them twice, but they only sent my letter from one place to another and did nothing to help. They kept saying we had to go to Qu'Appelle.

When I was dying, I told my people to stop here in the hills. I told them, "Don't you ever leave this land." They listened to me; they still remember my words.

C.S.: How do you feel about those white men, back then, who—

CHIEF N.: [interrupts, with a wave of his hand] You want to know more, you go talk to my great-great-granddaughter-in-law, Piyêso kâ-pêtowitak, that Jean Oakes. She's a good one for knowing these old stories. Hai hai.

If the goal of the reserve system had been to get Aboriginal people out of the settlers' way and keep the two groups apart, the authorities have clearly succeeded beyond all expectation. Almost a century and a half after the signing of the treaties, we still live for the most part in weirdly separate worlds, with decades of mistrust, sharp as razor wire, in between us. The forced settlement of treaty people had signaled the beginning of a traumatic period of authoritarian

misrule, marked by continuing hunger, the withholding of
agricultural technology (on the pretext that Indians needed
to start with hand tools and work their way up, through the
ages and stages of human development), the criminalization
of important ceremonies, virtual imprisonment under the
pass system, and the confinement of Aboriginal children in
residential-school hells. All these projects were initiated in
the 1880s by our old friend Whitebeard and his crack team
of bureaucrats and advisers.

How Aboriginal people must despise us, I thought, as I
reviewed these events. How bitter must be their resentment.
And here I was, about to ask for guidance and assistance.

The white man wants to give little and take much, Sitting Bull had once said, and I had no desire to follow in those
well-worn footsteps. If it were ever possible to establish a
connection with someone from the late Chief Nekaneet's
community who was willing to teach me—someone who
could offer me a glimpse of this eloquent landscape from
a different point of view—then I was determined to give
something of value in return. But what that something
might look like (a family history? a video? an archive of
interviews?) was impossible to predict, since there had to be
a meeting of minds before anything could happen.

Through Keith's circle of acquaintances at the university, I'd recently been introduced to an Aboriginal scholar
who is a respected authority on the preservation and sharing of indigenous knowledge. Her advice, though willing
and gentle, did nothing to quell my fears. In the first place,
she confirmed something I already suspected: I would
need official permission from chief and council before con-
ducting any "research." What's more, given the history of
exploitation—including the misappropriation of traditional

knowledge by commercial interests, with no reciprocal benefits– she advised me to direct any and all proceeds from my project to the community as recompense. Finally, there was also a case to be made for shared authorship between me and my hoped-for teachers and collaborators.

This was honorable council but, ouch, it carried a sting. What about little old me? I found myself wondering. Assuming that I was able to produce a publishable manuscript out of my accumulation of scribbled notes and untidy files, didn't I also merit some kind of sufficiency? As for authorial credit, would anyone else choose to lend his or her name to a work-in-progress that was almost certain to be personal, bumbling, and eccentric? Perhaps the present was so deeply contaminated by the miseries of the past that it was no longer possible to create a connection based on respect and trust, with a sharing of benefits among equals.

Months passed, and my letter to the chief and council of the Nekaneet First Nation went unanswered. Phone calls were not returned, and I began to prepare myself for the inevitable. But then one afternoon, as Keith and I were driving out to visit our horses in their pasture west of town, I pulled out my cell phone to make a last-ditch attempt. And, bingo, there's the chief on the line, and, yes, she will be happy to meet with me in her office on the reserve a few days hence.

"You know how to get here?" she asks me.

"No problem," I say, buoyed by this small success. "Thanks a lot, Chief Pahtayken. See you then."

Yeah, sure. No problem. Turns out that Nekaneet First Nation is not marked on any standard road map, and even Google is uncharacteristically reticent about its whereabouts. Still, the first leg of the trip is familiar, so off I set: west from Eastend to Ravenscrag, then north and west and north again through tawny, late-summer hills. Spinning over Top of the World Hill with its magnificent blue distance. Plunging through the deep gully where great blue herons teeter on the tippy-tops of dying cottonwood trees. Pausing to watch as fifteen, sixteen, seventeen white-tailed deer levitate over fences and across the pavement. Then it's up and over the summit and down into Maple Creek.

That's where things get dicey. The only available guidance comes from a narrow slat tacked to a fencepost on the eastern outskirts of town, which carries the faint legend "Nekaneet, 37 km." Unfortunately, the sign has lost its bearings and points listlessly to the ground. Still, the gravel road to the south and west looks promising, and the reserve has to be somewhere around here. A question mark hangs over every turning in the road, but for the next half hour or so, I cling to the main route, before literally coming to an impasse. The road has come to a stop at a T-junction. Turn to the right—but, no, that doesn't get me anywhere. What about this driveway? Edge past the cow in the middle of the track, don't mind the junk, ignore the yard of yapping dogs. Halloo, anyone home? A hand-lettered sign on the door of a trailer tells me all I need to know. It reads: *dangeras.*

Boy, am I ever lost!

"You mean you don't know where you are?" the young woman at the band office asks, when I get through to her by phone. The tone of her voice speaks volumes: how could anybody be so completely clueless? And she's right in more ways than she probably suspects. Though only a few miles off the highway, I'm a thousand miles out of my comfort zone. Should I have brought tobacco for the chief? Or should it have been cloth? I've lived on the prairies all my life. Surely, it shouldn't be this nerve-wracking to visit the neighbors.

The voice on the phone has me sorted out in an instant— turns out I'm almost there—and soon I'm parked in front of

the band office (a worn-looking brown shed), under the fluttering blue and white of the Treaty 4 flag. The chief leads
me into a spartan room, listens to my proposal, nods, and
then proceeds to pour out her heart. She talks about emotional trauma and its links to disease, about alcoholism and
wasted lives, about poverty and a father who taught her how
to survive. How to grow a garden; how to look after cattle;
how to snare and hunt different animals. "There is more to
life than money," she says several times. What truly matters,
she insists, is survival and health. "I know my community
isn't healthy." Instead of the suspicion and principled misgivings that I had expected, the chief is apparently prepared
to take me at my word. An hour into our conversation, she
stands up, leads me to another room, interrupts a meeting
in progress, introduces me to the band council, and says
that I will be visiting the reserve to speak to some of the
elders. Simple as that, I'm in, and it will be up to me to make
sure that something good comes of this.

JEAN OAKES and I meet in prison, though thankfully neither of us is confined behind bars. A cheerful, round-faced
woman in her late sixties, with metal-rimmed glasses, a
calm, reassuring manner, and a ready laugh, she perfectly
fills the role of grandmother. So it is fitting that she is
employed in that capacity, as elder, or *kokhum*, at the Okimaw Ohci Healing Lodge, a minimum-security correctional
institution for federally sentenced Aboriginal women.
Opened in 1995, the lodge occupies a cluster of comfortable, low-rise buildings in a stand of poplars on the highest
height of the Nekaneet reserve, fifteen minutes up the road
from the band office. In case you're wondering, as I was, the
lodge's website defines "healing for Aboriginal women" as
"the opportunity through Aboriginal teachings, programs,

spirituality and culture, to recover from histories of abuse, regain a sense of self-worth, gain skills and rebuild families." Although Aboriginal women make up three percent of the Canadian population, they constitute thirty-two percent of federally sentenced female prisoners, a statistic that speaks to a history of suffering.

Following a chain of acquaintances that had begun with the band council, I had ended up being invited, first, to attend a Horse Dance ceremony on a grassy meadow just above the lodge—a bright swirl of sunlight, drumming hooves, and prayers—and, now, to look in on a program that has been designed to assist selected "residents" with their "healing journeys." As each woman introduces herself in turn, she takes a moment either to reflect on a ceremony the group had held the day before or, even more poignantly, to grieve over the pain of being separated from her children. Just as the last of the tears is being dried away, the door edges open, and a short, grandmotherly figure slips in and sits down beside me.

"I was lucky I came from poor," she says, by way of introducing herself. "It was good that time, no alcohol, no drugs. Everybody used to be helping one another." Lucky to have been poor? That's not something you often hear. And when the class is adjourned for lunch, look at the way the "girls" crowd around her, teasing and asking for hugs. Might there be room for me inside that circle of affection?

A few weeks later, over an offering of tobacco—I'm learning!—I visit Kokhum Jean in her home (a neat white bungalow on a small knoll across from the band office) and do my best to explain why I've come. I tell her about arriving in Eastend and our old van and all the breakdowns and how, as we dangled from the umpteenth tow truck, we got the impression that something was telling us to stop and pay attention to where we were. I watch her out of the corner of my eye, in case she thinks I'm unhinged, but instead she looks pleased and nods in agreement.

"That is how we—." She breaks off, as if she too is uncertain how much it is safe to divulge. "That means you are supposed to be here," she continues. "This is your home. *Something* there is that is always watching us."

I tell her that I've been learning about the history of First Nations people in the Cypress Hills, and her response is matter of fact. "How does that make you feel? Angry?" she asks. If she is angry herself, it doesn't show in her voice. Still, my heart blenches with the realization that though it has come as news to me, she and other indigenous people have known the truth from the beginning.

Here I am, a *moonias* from the city who has turned up out of the blue to ask for teaching and help. Yet like the chief and council before her, Jean has literally and figuratively opened her door to my request. Yes, she will tell me what she knows about Chief Nekaneet and about what happened back then. Better yet, she will also accept my help in making her own book of teachings and recollections for her children and grandchildren. (*Stories From My Life,* by Jean Francis Oakes, was published in 2008.) Instead of the bitterness and resentment I had feared and half-believed I deserved, my presence seems to have been accepted as one of nature's little whims, like the wild lupines along the road that cuts through the reserve or a bird that has landed on a windowsill.

And so the storytelling begins. We sit at her kitchen table, amid moccasins-in-progress and piles of brightly colored beads. Way back, she tells me, there were four large reserves in the Cypress Hills, or so her parents and grandparents had said. "Lucky I used to be nosy," she interjects merrily. "That's why I know all these stories. I was the oldest, I had to watch the baby. Sometimes I'd just pretend to be watching the babies so I could hear what was going on." Her kitchen rings with laughter.

"My chief, Nekaneet, he was stubborn. Even with them telling him like that, 'You're going to be starving here if you don't move,' he still didn't give in. 'Even if they kill me, you guys don't move,' he was telling his band members. They moved the other people all away. That's why we are all alone.

"And after that our reserve was small, small, shaped like an *L*."

Jean breaks off, puts on the kettle, and I think of what I've read about what happened next. In 1913, with the Dewdney-era bureaucrats finally out of the picture and with pressure now coming not only from the "stragglers" (as the government described the Nekaneet people) but from concerned settlers as well, Indian Affairs finally relented and created a token reserve. Instead of the quality cropland and pastures the chiefs had selected and that they thought had been given to them, the new Maple Creek reserve consisted of 1,440 acres (nine quarter-sections) of rough wooded land, miles from the nearest town, to support a community of eighty-one men, women, and children. "We are absolutely destitute," a spokesman for the group informed Ottawa the following autumn, "and without some assistance from your department it will be impossible for us to live." [6] But except for an admonition to try harder and the promise of a miserly ration for those in deadly distress, Indian Affairs remained unresponsive to appeals for help. The band (under the leadership of Jean's late husband, Gordon) would have to wait until 1992 to receive compensation for the additional 16,160 acres to which they were entitled by the terms of Treaty 4. A claim for other treaty benefits, also long withheld, was finally settled in November 2009.

It was during the difficult early years on the reserve that groups of Nekaneet people sometimes drove their horse-drawn wagons over to Eastend and camped in the river brush, where they were surreptitiously observed by a boy named Wallace. "Probably they were Cree," he later noted; "undoubtedly they came from some reservation, though it never occurred to us to inquire where it was; probably they were off the reservation without permission. We responded to them as to an invasion or a gypsy visitation . . .

"We told ourselves we could smell one of those camps a mile away with a clothespin on our noses," he remembered. "When they talked the butcher out of the entrails of a slaugh-tered beef we knew we could, for they hung their shanties with the red and white guts to dry them in the sun."[7] He believed that he was witnessing the last days of a vanish-ing race. But red and white are good colors, the colors of north and south. Sometimes, just to survive is a magnificent achievement.

Like their chief before them, the Nekaneet people were stubborn, and they knew how to get by. "I was lucky I came from a poor way," Jean says again, as she returns to the table and hands me a mug of tea. "We used to be the workers, my two brothers and me. We used to go to sleep early, get up at five in the morning already. Go feed the horses. You make a fire. My mom already will be cooking. And we'd go in the bush, not even light yet, make fence posts, chopping wood. That's how we used to do it, how we used to survive."

I think of my dying mother speaking of her mother before her: all those babies, hell on earth. But Jean is not downhearted. "That was good that time," she says, a con-tented purr in her voice. "Me, I never got tired of working."

IF THERE is one blot on Jean's childhood memories, it is not poverty or constant labor or the burdens of history. It is her lack of formal schooling. "Lots of times it hurt me, I don't have no education," she laments. "Sometimes you feel this short." She squeezes a narrow slit between thumb and forefinger.

It wasn't that her elders were opposed to learning; the problem was that they knew too much. Many of them had been victims of the residential-school system. (The first Indian industrial school opened on the prairies in 1883, with the unabashed intent of "killing the Indian" in its students.) "They used to pull their ears and hit them with wooden sticks if they spoke a word of Cree," Jean says, her voice rising with disbelief. Another time, she whispers, "These nuns and preachers, they used to treat girls bad. The nuns would be holding the girls, and the priests there. That's what Josephine [her husband's aunt] told us later. 'The nuns, they hold me and the priests would force themselves.' Josephine told us what happened."

That's when Jean looks up, glimpses the pain in my eyes, and offers what comfort she can. "It's not you that got treated bad that time." Her elders were so determined to protect their children that they managed to enlist the help of the local mounted police officer. "When the wagon came from Lebret [a residential school in the Qu'Appelle Valley], someone would call that policeman—Fleming his name was, Sergeant David Fleming Senior—and he would come in his black pants and red coat. He used to tell them, 'Leave those Nekaneet alone. They don't want their kids to go to school.' Two generations, we didn't go to school, my mom and me."

ALTHOUGH JEAN was deprived of schooling, she was certainly not untaught. Her "good teachers" were her parents and grandparents—"real traditional people," she calls

them—and the knowledge that they imparted to her sometimes makes me catch my breath. Despite all the trouble
they knew in their lives, they remembered who they were
and the teachings they had received from their own elders.
For instance, Jean and I might be having a completely ordinary conversation about her ancestry (a great-grandmother
from Montana; a beloved *mosom,* or grandpa, who was born
on Red Pheasant reserve and joined the community through
marriage) when she'd calmly add that one of her great-grand-
fathers was a healer who had "come from the Thunders."

"That Sawepiton, he came from Thunder," she'd say.
"That's what he used to tell us. And one time, the Thunders, his dad, told him you are going to go to the Middle of
the earth. That's why he used to know everything. All what
they do here now, all these songs, these ceremonies, they got
from him. We got a lot of good history from my mosom."

She remembers how she and the other kids would beg
him for stories—"He was a storyteller, just like a radio"—but
if it was summertime, he would always say no. "'No, I'm not
going to tell you. It would make it cold.'"

"I used to always be happy when it was cold so my mosom
could tell us stories and talk about Wesa'kaca." Those were
still her favorites, the trickster stories of Wesa'kaca, filled
with mischief, mayhem, and good humor.

One day, several months into our acquaintance, Jean
decides to tell me about the Healing Lodge and why it is
located on the Nekaneet reserve. "My old man, Gordon, he
knows for a long time ago there's going to be something
there for women," she begins. "He used to dream he had a
sweat up there on that hill and there's lots of ladies—they
are all laughing, they are happy—but he didn't know why. He
used to dream about that for four years before. I guess that's
meant to be there."

Okimaw Ohci, that's "a good word," she continues, "but nobody says it right. They say okima oki. That's like your bum." She frowns. "Oh-keema-wo-chee," she says firmly. "That's like Kink Hill."

Kink Hill?

"Wesa'kaca, that's okimaw, that's our king."

Oh, King Hill!

"Just like the white people had Jesus over there. In the old country, they had a hill like that. Jesus and Wesa'kaca are the same kind.

"That one, Wesa'kaca he used to heal people; he used to tell us in the future what's going to happen. He made this world. You remember that story? Everything was flooded—there was just a little place to stand on, and all the people were there. And they send down one animal and another one, to try to go get dirt from under the water. Muskrat, he was the one who went and got that dirt, under his fingernail, and Wesa'kaca took that dirt and blew on it. That's how he made the land get bigger. Pretty soon it was growing. And that time now, he sent Coyote to measure the land.

"'Go check how big the country is now.' And I guess that Coyote was just old when he came back."

She pauses, her round face alight with contentment. "Oh, it makes me happy to hear those good stories," she says.

"Wesa'kaca made the world here, you know that? That's why there are all the hills here. He used to point like this,"—she stretches out a hand—"'You, I'm going to make you.'"

And when his world was finished, "that hill is where Wesa'kaca was sitting, the one they call the meadow where the Healing Lodge is now. You know, where they had that Horse Dance?"

Do I know it? I was there; I stood on that holy ground. I can feel my eyes go wide as saucers.

"That Wesa'kaca, he was sitting there singing, and he was telling people, 'I'm going to leave you guys now, my brothers and my sisters. I'm going to go now.' Wesa'kaca was telling us, 'I'm going to go now. But I'll still watch you guys when you are here.'

"Here," she says, with a gesture that extends beyond the walls of her house to sweep over the hills and the plains beyond, "there is something that pulls you, something that makes you want to stay. I always think maybe it's that Wesa'kaca. He's still got the power; he's still watching us, not to be lonely. You never hear anyone say here, 'I am lonely.'"

ELEVEN

HOME TRUTH

Wisdom sits in places.
It's like water that never dries up.
You need to drink water to stay alive, don't you?
Well, you also need to drink from places.
You must remember everything about them.
You must learn their names.
You must remember what happened at them long ago.
You must think about it and keep on thinking about it.
Then your mind will become smoother and smoother.
Then you will see danger before it happens.

DUDLEY PATTERSON, Apache elder, 1996

IN ALL the times I've told the story of Keith's and my arrival in Eastend, there was one essential detail that, for the longest time, I completely forgot. Like an unconformity in the geological strata, it was simply gone, as absent as if it had never happened. Then one day, some time after my conversations with Jean had begun, the lost memory reappeared in full definition.

Before our first trip to Eastend, Keith and I had spent time in Cody, Wyoming, and it wasn't the legend of Buffalo Bill that had drawn us in. Instead, we had gone there to attend an educational program, one of a now lamentably discontinued series of seminars on "Plains Indian" cultures, this one on the theme of the sacred landscapes of the Great Plains. For three intense days, we'd sat in a basement room at the Buffalo Bill Historical Center and listened as a roster of scholars and activists from the American West spoke about the struggle of traditional people to live in relationship with the land, as an act of renewal and remembrance.

"Hills are very mysterious places," a Piikáni elder named Curly Bear Wagner had said. "That's what we mean by sacred. Mysterious."

Now, leafing through my notes from the conference, I am astonished to see that they read like a how-to manual for the encounter that lay ahead, with a town I had never been to, a house I had no thought to buy, and a range of hills that until then had scarcely caught my eye. If I had set out purposefully to develop a curriculum for my travels in the Cypress Hills, I could not have done any better than this. ("How do you know places," one speaker had asked, "unless you know the names and the stories they have to tell?") And then I erased these insights from my conscious thoughts as if they had nothing to do with me or with the unknown future I was entering.

Funny the things we remember, the things we choose to forget. Funny the way we keep finding ourselves at the beginning again.

IT'S TEN years and counting since Keith and I blew into town for what was supposed to be a two-week stay, an end-of-summer flourish of fun and frolic. Surely no one could have predicted that this lyrical country would, gradually, patiently, over time, begin to reveal its secrets to me, an accidental pilgrim who didn't even know what she was seeking.

"Not to be lonely," Jean had said. That is what has always drawn people to the Cypress Hills. And as I reflect on what she has told me, I can't help but wonder if, long before Keith and I arrived here, we might have been suffering unwittingly from a species of loneliness. If there are varieties of religious experience, à la William James, might there not also be varieties of disconnection? I'm not thinking of an aloneness that can be soothed by intimacy—and Keith so alive and so well—or even of the lost-in-the-crowd-ness that we sometimes felt in the city and that yielded so readily to the easy, open-hearted friendliness of a rural community.

But what if, beyond our need for one another, we humans also have an urgent, inarticulate need for the more-than-human world? Whether or not that world has a spiritual dimension is a subject I'll have to leave to you. What I can talk about with more assurance are the everyday mysteries of wind and rain, fish and fowl, winter-spring-summer-and-fall, all things wild and wonderful. Clearly, there are many people who don't get in a flutter, as Keith and I always do, about every little living thing that comes into view—the lilting flight of a kingfisher along the river behind our house or a shiny new bee in the bergamot beside our back door.

But I defy you to find anyone so deadened that he or she could glimpse the honey-slow movements of a cougar just up ahead on the path, not five minutes' walk from the T.rex Centre and only fifteen minutes from our house, without standing tingling and breathless as it soft-foots it through the snow and, with many a backward glance, flows out of sight in the underbrush. And surely no one could lie on the rim of the Frenchman Valley with a night chill in the air and gaze out into that great swirling river of stars without finding him- or herself a fallen star in the grass, alight with satisfaction and wonderment.

Way back when tyrannosaurs ruled this valley, which wasn't a valley yet, the starlight that fell on their retinas was already ancient. And when the brontotheres squinted up through their piggy eyes, many millions of years afterwards, the minute hand of the cosmic clock had barely ticked forward. The universe is unfathomably old, and life on earth is young, the creative exuberance of a split second. On the time scale of the cosmos, human beings have existed for an eye blink, and here on the plains, in particular, all of our storied history—from the moment of creation, through the long reign of the buffalo prairie, to the trauma of colonization—press in upon the present. The past is as close as a circle of stones on the prairie, the fractured skull of a buffalo protruding from a creek, a friend sitting in her kitchen with her beadwork and telling good old stories about creation and a meadow just up the way.

ALL OF our storied history. In April of 1885, not long after the Cree and Nakoda had been deported from the Cypress Hills, a reporter with the *Toronto Daily Mail* arrived at the Maple Creek train station. The racial tension that had crackled around the Cypress Hills for the preceding decade had been dispersed by the ethnic clearance, but it had never been defused. Now, it had ignited into violence. That spring, the firepower of the Canadian state would be marshaled against an ad hoc militia of Métis civilians, fighting for land rights and recognition, and against scattered resistance by treaty people—including members of Big Bear's still-homeless band—who remained on the verge of despair and starvation.

Despite a few early reversals, the outcome would never be seriously in doubt. By autumn, the Macdonald government would celebrate its victory with a row of eight Aboriginal corpses dangling from gallows on a hill at Battleford, the last and one of the largest public executions ever conducted on Canadian soil. (As Prime Minister Macdonald explained in a private note to Dewdney, "The executions . . . ought to convince the Red Man that the White Man governs."[1]) Métis leader Louis Riel was executed privately in Regina, and several prominent treaty chiefs, including the peace-talking Big Bear, were convicted of treason and locked up in Stony Mountain Penitentiary, the closest thing to a death sentence. If the incomer and Aboriginal communities ever do begin to talk sincerely about how the West was won, we are going to have a lot of painful ground to cover.

But to get back to our reporter, last seen disembarking from Sir John A.'s railroad onto the platform at Maple Creek. He's made the five-hour journey from Swift Current—through a landscape deeply etched with buffalo trails and strewn with their "numberless skeletons"—with the mundane objective of purchasing a saddle horse. By the time we catch up with him, he has completed this transaction (a small triumph, since the military had snapped up most of the serviceable horseflesh in the country and put it to urgent use) and is on the lookout for people to interview. The next day finds him riding out ten miles east of town, with a translator, toward a cluster of canvas tipis on the banks of Piapot Creek.

At the approach of the visitors, someone runs for the chief—out planting potatoes, we're told. He's an impressive sight, "fully six feet two . . . [and] straight as an arrow," clad in a blue blanket, with brass rings in his earlobes, brass beads on his long braids, and the remains of a top hat, ringed with feathers, crowning his head. His name is Nekaneet.

"I have come from the home of my people beyond the great lakes to see the Indians and to talk with them," the reporter says. "I want to know about the grievances of the Indians and half-breeds, so that I can tell all the people about them." As if anyone really cared. As if the population of Ontario weren't already crying for vengeance against the traitors.

But Nekaneet accepts the offer at face value and, accompanied by members of his council, invites the visitor into a tipi, smokes the pipe with him, and recalls the painful story of the displacement of his people. His words are familiar. "Colonel Irvine said the Great Mother had given this land to us and marked it with a pile of stones. It was to be for us and our children.

"But already the white men have come in," he continues, with a sweeping gesture. "Their tipis are there now, on the place that was to be for us. You can see them." He pauses for translation and to let his emotions settle.

"We are hungry," he says quietly. "Where are the buffalo? Where are our horses? They are gone, and we must soon follow them. Your people have our land. These prairies were ours once, and the buffalo were given us by the Great Spirit. They kept us warm; they kept us from being hungry; they kept us in fuel. But all are gone.

"Surely the rich white people, who are as numberless as the blades of grass upon the prairie or the leaves upon the trees in the Cypress Hills, can help their red brothers. When a white man came amongst us when I was a boy we fed him, warmed him, and gave him horses for his journey. Why don't they do the same for us now?

"Perhaps they would if they knew. But the [Indian] agents have two tongues, and our white brothers far away think we are not hungry. They think we are happy. But look at me, look at those round me, and say, do we look happy? Are these blankets warm enough for the winter? Are they like the buffalo robes we used to have?

"Let them take back the blankets and return the buffalo robes. Let them send the buffalo back, and take their own people to the reserve where they came from. Give us the prairies again and we won't ask for food." The chief looks down at his calloused hands, his worn-out moccasins.

"It is too late," he says finally. "The iron road has frightened the game away, and the talking wire stretches from sunrise to sunset. It is too late." He pauses, and there is no mistaking the pain in his eyes. "It is too late," he says again. But then he picks up his axe and, still daring to hope, goes back to planting potatoes.[2]

IT IS Hard Time Moon, January 2010, and Keith (who has remained an ever-present if increasingly silent partner in this adventure since I became overwhelmed by the past) stands shivering on the edge of our snow-banked driveway in Eastend, engulfed in clouds of breath as he runs through his standard list of cautions. Drive carefully. Full tank of gas? Watch out for slippery roads. But really, he needn't worry. If there's one thing these hills have taught us, it is to stay alert. And it's not just the seasonal round of road hazards—whether black ice or potholes or slithery muck—that one has to watch out for. There are also the unsigned distractions of the past. This country is filled with ghosts that leap out of the coulees, fleshy and unexpected as deer, and almost as likely, in their own way, to cause a derailment.

Today's journey, from our house in the Frenchman Valley to the Healing Lodge on the Nekaneet First Nation's land, will take less than two hours but will span hundreds of thousands of years. As I nose our new pickup down the street (the longer we spend in Eastend, the more country we become), my thoughts are already running up and over the rim of the valley—north, south, east, and west—to map a route through this landscape of remembrance. First, an X to mark this silent street asleep under drifts of snow. *Voici les neiges d'antan,* the snows of my childhood. A block to the south, there's the Stegner House and the memories it holds of people who thought they were Adam and Eve in a new and unstoried world. And overlooking the town and its follies, more dots appear on the map. The bones of long-extinct monsters in the T.rex Centre just above our house. A fossilized seashell half-buried in the dust. A cluster of tipi rings, shoulder-deep in the grass, that tell their story with stony eloquence.

Draw a conflagration at Chimney Coulee. Place a question mark over the site of the purported Crazy Horse refugee camp. And as the highway leads us west and north, let the map spool out beyond the reach of today's travel toward Fort Walsh—with a cannon at each gate—and the field of slaughter at Whitemud Coulee. Watch as the Nakoda bid farewell to their murdered kinsfolk and begin the painful trek toward the Skull Mountainettes. Mark the starvation camp at Cypress Lake with a death's head. "It is too late," Nekaneet had said. He knew there was trouble ahead.

Now, scribble in the road that lurches from the outskirts of Maple Creek up to the Healing Lodge. Buzz yourself through the gate and again through the heavy front doors. Surrender your keys and your phone at the office. Fasten a panic button to your belt. Ask yourself what, in heaven's name, made you to agree to come back to prison again.

In a tiny room down a hallway, half a dozen "residents" are crowded around a table, waiting for class to begin. At the far end sits a friendly looking Aboriginal woman with a cheerful laugh, who extends her hand and introduces herself. On first acquaintance, you would never guess that she is a repeat drunk driver responsible for the deaths of six people in a horrific accident. The pretty girl beside her, with the perky updo and the star tattooed on her cheek, is serving time for armed robbery. Next, an incorrigible addict and drug dealer, as bright and chatty as they come, and then a soft-voiced, sad-eyed girl who is known on the street by the gangster name of Shady. And so it goes, all around the room. You could be forgiven for thinking that these women are nothing but trouble.

The purpose of the class is to teach these unlikely students to conduct and transcribe interviews, skills they may be able to use when they return to their home reserves. (With the publication of Jean's book, I have unexpectedly become the local go-to person on oral-history research.) And how better to encourage my protégées to practice these techniques than by encouraging them to tell one another their own life stories?

You might think that, given everything the hills had taught me, I would have known what to expect. But it is one thing to witness a catastrophe from a distance and quite another to sit with its aftermath in a crowded room, up close and personal. Although every woman's story is different, it quickly becomes clear that they are all heroic survivors, born into the same shattered world.

"Both my mother and grandmother were alcoholics."

"She grabbed the wooden broom and started to hit me."

"The age of eleven, I got sexually abused."

"I was raped."

"I never realized I had been stabbed."

"He came into the house with an axe and was threatening my mother with it."

"I wanted to numb all my pain that I was feeling inside."

"I did just about anything to feed my addiction."

"I am not making any excuses for what has happened in my life."

"A lot of pain created me to end up here."

And something else that almost made me cry. The girl with the star on her cheek had been born in the same city and the very same hospital where my own girl was born. Our stories were interwoven, all of us caught in the web of everything that had ever happened.

SOMETIMES, DRIVING back through the hills after one of my visits to the Healing Lodge, I'd find myself thinking about those two women who, for going on fifty years, had been standing stock still on opposite sides of a different meadow. One of them, my grandmother, had a face and a name, Pauline Sherk née Jaque, but what about the anonymous figure in buckskin and braids on the far shore of the clearing? Was it too late to make some kind of connection with her? There was only one person I could think of who might be able to help, and that was my dad's cousin, Nora, up north in the Peace River Country. For one thing, I'd always adored her, with her friendly moon face and a voice that always seemed on the verge of bubbling over into laughter. For another, she had grown up on the Sherk Brothers homesteads, across the road from my dad and within walking distance of the Indian Quarter. Best of all, she is also the family historian.

"You know," Nora says thoughtfully when I get her on the phone, "I've always wondered about those people, too. And do you remember, in the fall, how the coyotes would be howling down there, along the river?" Now that she mentions it, I can imagine them moving in the green shadows and hear their tremulous song. "It was always kind of—" she pauses for a beat—"kind of mysterious. Why don't you give me a few days and I'll see what I can come up with?"

Sure enough, a week later the phone rings and there is Nora, with quite a story to tell. Turns out that, long before the "pioneers" arrived, the Indian Quarter had been a favorite river crossing and campsite on a well-traveled trail to the south and west, from the region of the *grande prairie* to the mountains. By the 1890s, a small cluster of log homes had been established at the crossing—"I seem to remember the folks saying that, in the early days, there were ten or twelve cabins down there"—and at least one of them was a permanent residence. It belonged to a Cree-speaking man named Patrick Joachim and his wife, Marie Joachim née Tranquille, and it was there, on the flats of the Beaverlodge River, that four of their children were born: son Albert in 1907; then two daughters, Mary Jane and Marie; and finally another son, Joseph, in 1917. (My dad was born just up the road a couple of years later.)

But while the Joachims were busy with their young family, events had been closing in on them. The national ambitions that had steamrolled across the Great Plains on both sides of the Canada–U.S. border and that had side-swiped the Cypress Hills were now advancing farther north. The first move came at the turn of the twentieth century with the signing of Treaty 8, which extinguished Aboriginal claims to about 320,000 square miles of forest and forest-fringe from what is now north-central Saskatchewan across Alberta to north-central B.C. A decade later, in 1910, the Canadian government unilaterally set aside a chunk of the Treaty 8 area as the new Jasper National Park, thereby dispossessing a group called the Mountain Métis, which included members of the Joachims' extended family. Suddenly homeless, these people were compensated for the loss of their buildings but not for their land, a grievance that has never been settled. (This story was starting to sound unpleasantly familiar.)

Meanwhile, back at the Beaverlodge crossing, another shakeup was taking place. The first wave of incomers had arrived in the area the previous autumn—the real deal, with oxen and covered wagons—and had spent the winter in tents. With spring, they fanned out over the countryside and began the herculean task of proving up on their homesteads. My great-grandparents, grandfather, and great-uncle (Nora's dad) were among them.

Nora pauses, and I can hear her fingers rustling through her stack of documents. "Here's the part that kind of bothers me," she says. In 1914, ringed in by incomers and perhaps chastened by the plight of his kinsfolk, Patrick Joachim had decided to apply for formal title to his home. His claim was made—Nora has found what she was looking for and is now reading from Joachim's text—"'by virtue of the occupation of the land at the time of extinguishment of [Aboriginal] title.'

"And listen to this," she continues. "It almost made me cry. 'As I was in peaceful possession of this land at the time of the Treaty in 1899—'

"*As I was in peaceful possession*—" she begins again. "And you know, even after that, he had to wait three whole years to get the title to his land." Once the paperwork was completed, Patrick Joachim almost immediately sold out to

Leon Ferguson, who eventually sold on to the Sherks. The Joachims are said to have joined Métis communities elsewhere in Alberta or in B.C., but there is no trace of them in Beaverlodge pioneer histories.

"The Sherks and the Joachims lived right side by side for—what?—a good seven, eight years," Nora says, her voice rising with surprise. "But all the time I was growing up, I never heard the folks mention them. Not even once. Doesn't that strike you as odd?"

My mind flashes back to the two vague, frozen figures who have haunted me for so long. But to my surprise, though the trail and the grass and the river remain, the ghosts have gone. Instead, I see two women at a table strewn with brightly colored beads. Two women at a table, talking.

THERE'S ONE more place I want to take you before I bring this runaway steed to a halt. It goes by the unromantic name of the Stampede Site, and to find it, you simply let your mind wander straight west from Okimaw Ohci, past Fort Walsh and over the Alberta-Saskatchewan line, toward the highest height of the hills at what used to be called the Head of the Mountain. There, on land that was once home to the Niitsítapi, then promised to the Nakoda, and finally incorporated into Cypress Hills Interprovincial Park, you will find the picturesque resort town of Elkwater, Alberta, and a series of signposts that direct you to an event at the local rodeo grounds.

It's June, and the place is abuzz with school kids who have been bused in from near and far for a celebration called "History in the Hills." The main attraction is an array of glowing white tipis, some painted and others plain, that are dotted across a grassy field. Off to one side, there's a portly little bell tent, of the kind once used by the North-West Mounted Police, and a couple of four-walled trappers' tents. One of them has a Red River cart parked beside it. Métis fiddle tunes alternate with the throb of powwow songs, and from inside several of the tipis, a low murmur of voices is heard, as the children (mostly the descendants of incomers) listen to speakers from the Cree, Nakoda, Siksika, and Métis nations. Meanwhile, on the edge of the clearing, a red-coated police officer bellows cheerful commands as he puts his intake of pint-sized recruits through their paces.

But we haven't come here for these festivities, as inviting as they are. Instead, our destination is a stand of aspens—a shimmer of tender spring green—that is just visible on the opposite side of the field. Here, in a dazzle of sunshine, we have an unusual chance to gaze directly into the depths of the past. At our feet lies an enormous sheer-sided pit, big enough to swallow a house. Almost thirty feet on a side and twenty feet deep, it was dug by archaeologists, trowel and dustpan in hand, over six summers in the early 2000s. Like the cliffs along the Ravenscrag road in miniature, the walls of this human-made crater are striated with light and dark, reminders that the earth is constantly inconstant. Light-colored layers represent wet spells, when a nearby creek flooded its banks and covered the ground with silt. Dark bands represent dry times, when soil accumulated. There is even a deposit of ash from a volcano far to the south that spewed debris across the plains thousands of years ago.

Yet no matter what happened, whether floods or droughts or tectonic ruptures, bands of buffalo-hunting people kept coming here to camp. They were here eight thousand years ago, when someone dropped a bone needle—as white as ivory and as delicate as a stem of grass—on ground that now lies twenty feet beneath the surface. They were here seven thousand years later, when someone else put down a stone awl, its surface polished smooth as glass, and forgot to pick it up again. In all, the site has yielded nearly a million artifacts, going back almost nine thousand years and documenting the repeated presence of people in this place over hundreds of generations.

Each generation followed in the footsteps of those who had gone before. In fact, new arrivals sometimes situated their camps on the very same spot their ancestors had used in the past, whether ten or a hundred or five hundred years before them. The Stampede Site has recorded this act of remembrance as a sequence of subtle basins, or hearths, filled with charcoal and bone, each one stacked directly on top of the one below. It appears that the buffalo people had a relationship with this place that they maintained by visiting it, almost as if it were a person.

It just so happens that on this particular June day in the twenty-first century, during "History in the Hills," a group of thoroughly modern people has come here in the hope of renewing this ancient connection. A mixed party of students, instructors, and elders from the Niitsítapi Teacher Education Program, they cluster around one end of the excavation and listen as an archaeologist explains what this research has revealed. When the thousand-year-old awl is passed around, the guy standing beside me murmurs that he has seen that same ultra-smooth finish before, on objects in Káínai medicine bundles. Curious, I look up to see a tallish man with deep-set eyes, graying temples, and a ball cap perched on his head. He introduces himself as Narcisse.

I'm not sure who had originally told me about Narcisse Blood and his mission to reconnect with the sacred landscape of the Niitsítapi. But there's no doubt about it: here he is, in the flesh. Later that same day, I manage to distract him for a moment from his duties as co-leader of the teacher-training class to offer him tobacco and ask for help. I run through my usual routine about tow trucks and being called to attention. I tell him about the new version of the "pioneer" story that I've been required to learn, one that acknowledges the violence that was done both to the buffalo prairie and to its human inhabitants—to the people who were settled here long before "settlement" began. But what was I still missing? What were these hills trying to tell me that I still couldn't hear? Might he have time to clue me in?

For a long moment, Narcisse doesn't answer. Then, just as I'm about to break the silence—"Of course, there's no reason . . . I perfectly understand—" he tips his cap to the back of his head and surprises me with a yes. "How do you deal with the grief?" he says, his gaze fixed on something that I cannot see. "It is really a very short time since contact—a hundred years is a long time, but not in Blackfoot time, not in buffalo time . . ."

He pauses and looks at me. "The knowledge that was here in this land for thousands of years has been ignored," he continues, his voice matter of fact. "You can't be sustained without knowledge of the land. What we're talking about here is survival."

There's just one catch to Narcisse's offer of assistance. To understand the Cypress Hills, he says that it's not enough to know them in isolation, as an island apart. They have to be seen in relationship with other sacred places. I can feel my ears prick like a coyote's. What on earth is he talking about? "That's when you begin to understand that the renewal stopped for a reason," he goes on, weaving a web of meanings I don't immediately grasp. "That's when you begin to see that a lot of knowledge can be recovered, from the Blackfoot language and from the land. Even though, yes, a lot has been lost, it's not too late for things to start again. We have to begin thinking about our nonhuman relations."

So it's in a state of bewildered anticipation a few weeks later that I find myself in company with Narcisse again, making the rounds of sacred places in southern Alberta. At Head-Smashed-In Buffalo Jump, he tells me that the "stopping" of the buffalo had caused famine not just for people but also for the land and for all the insects, birds, and mammals that relied on their great snuffling, dusty, shaggy abundance. The wolves, the vultures, the grizzly bears have lost their source of food, he says. The grasslands are no longer grazed as only the buffalo know how to do.

"It's a famine that the newcomers"—he means people like me—"are only beginning to sense, and not enough people are aware of it."

Then it's on to the Aakii piskaan, the Women's Buffalo Jump, near Cayley, and from there to Okotoks, where we pay a visit to a monumental, wing-shaped slab of quartzite that towers over bales in a hayfield. Every place we go, he tells me stories about Napi, Old Man, and his sacred, comic misadventures. Late afternoon finds us in the farthest reaches of a cow pasture scarified by natural-gas extraction—"These days, we have a very violent type economy," my companion says—overlooking the dark, sinuous valley of the Bow River. Behind us, the Majorville medicine wheel extends its twenty-eight spidery spokes to an enclosing circle of stones. Around us, a wide world of ochre and tan spirals out in every direction, and for a moment, I'm back home again along the Frenchman River. "How we are in these places," Narcisse will tell me later, "that's how we would be in the Cypress Hills if the connection hadn't been lost. Sometimes I think—like when you're on a hunger strike, there's a point of no return. But mostly I think the knowledge is still recoverable."

Whenever we're in the car traveling, Narcisse sits in the passenger seat and talks nonstop, retelling the good old stories that belong to these special places. "This is a storied landscape, a ceremonial landscape," he explains, as if aware that I'm struggling to keep up, "very alive with its spirits and beings." Whenever we stop to visit a site, he is quiet and relaxed—"Don't you feel welcome here?" he asks me more than once—and he always takes time to say a few words in Blackfoot. Once I hear my name and, without waiting to be asked, he explains that he has prayed for me and for this book.

"We come to these sites because our ancestors have prayed for us here," he tells me, "for the people who were not yet born. They prayed for us to survive, to do the things they had always done."

"Did they pray for people like me?" I voice this question timidly, not sure I want to know. "Do you think they will help me now?" I'm surprised to hear these words tumble out of my mouth.

For a long minute, he doesn't answer. "Yes, I think so," he says at last. "You made the effort, you came here. There is a lot more to know, but this is a good start." He flashes me a rueful grin. "Anyway, you newcomers are not going any-where, and we aren't going anywhere either. I think it's a viewpoint now of we're in this together."

This is a story that has to be marked: To Be Continued.

{ ACKNOWLEDGMENTS }

M Y ENCOUNTER with the Cypress Hills was made possible by the vision and dedication of the members
of the Eastend Arts Council, who not only own and
operate the Wallace Stegner House but who also, through
a variety of other initiatives, help to keep the creative fire
burning in southwestern Saskatchewan. Our time in Eastend has also been enriched by the company of Sharon Butala
and the late Peter Butala, Betty Davis and the late Bob Davis,
Dr. Anne Davis and Kevin Bristow, Susan Howard, Wendy
Kabrud, Bryson LaBoissiere, Sue Michalsky and Roland Bear,
Jim Saville, Mary Thomson, Seán Virgo, Ethel Wills, Sherry
Wright and Bill Caton, and Sherry and Dennis Webster, all of
whom have deepened my understanding of what it means to
be a prairie person.

If it takes a village to raise a child, it has taken an
extended community to nurture this story. Words cannot

adequately express my appreciation for the generosity of elder Jean Francis Oakes, Piyêso kâ-pêtowitak, of Nekaneet First Nation. We are all lucky that, as she puts it, she "used to be nosy." I was also privileged to consult with Dale Mosquito and Linda Oakes, also from Nekaneet, and with elder Harry Francis of Piapot First Nation. Thanks are due, as well, to former Nekaneet chief Alice Pahtayken and her council for permission to visit the reserve and to former school principal Trevor Bearance for helping me to get my bearings. Patrick Wallace, then assistant warden management services at the Okimaw Ohci Healing Lodge, opened many doors for me, and Clare McNab, ex-Kikawinaw at the lodge, made it possible to believe that telling the truth about the past could be a road to healing.

So many other people have helped me over the years that it is impossible to name them all. I owe a particular debt to family historian Nora Hassell of Grande Prairie, researcher Lou Lockhart of Saskatoon, and Royce Pettijohn and Clayton Y. Yarshenko, who are mainstays of the Southwest Saskatchewan Old Timers Museum in Maple Creek and of Fort Walsh (now the Fort Walsh and Cypress Hills Massacre national historic sites). Two First Nations art stars, visual artist Lori Blondeau and playwright Kenneth T. Williams, provided astute advice and encouragement when it was most needed. The book also benefited from the expert counsel of a number of scholars, including Barry Ahenakew, then chief of Ahtahkakoop First Nation, now with the Saskatchewan Indian Cultural Centre; Tim Tokaryk, T.rex Discovery Centre and Royal Saskatchewan Museum; the late John Tobias, Red Deer; Donalee Deck, Parks Canada; Dr. Marie Battiste, Dr. Margaret Kennedy, and Dr. David Meyer, University of Saskatchewan; Dr. David Sauchyn, University of Regina; Dr. Cynthia Chambers, University of Lethbridge; Dr. Alison

Landals, Stantec Consulting, Calgary; and Dr. Brian Reeves and Dr. Gerald Oetelaar, University of Calgary. In addition, I was inspired by speakers at "History in the Hills" in 2006 and 2007 (notably Val Ryder of the Carry the Kettle First Nation) and at seminars organized by the Buffalo Bill Historical Center in Cody, Wyoming, including Dr. Linea Sundstrom, Joe Medicine Crow, and the late Blackfeet cultural historian Curly Bear Wagner. As for the ebullient, eloquent Narcisse Blood of the Káínai Nation and Red Crow College, my admiration for his insight, mischievous humor, and kindness is unbounded.

It is an honor to acknowledge the endorsement of the David Suzuki Foundation and the financial support of the Saskatchewan Arts Board and the Canada Council for the Arts.

The book was reviewed in manuscript by editor Shelley Tanaka, novelist Suzanne North, and historians Dr. Bill Waiser and Dr. Sheena Rolph, each of whom offered valuable advice that was gratefully taken to heart. Keith Bell, my companion in all good things, listened patiently to passages read aloud, hot off the screen, and commented on several early drafts with a remarkable combination of insight and tact. Nancy Flight of Greystone Books provided editorial direction with professional vigor and grace, and publisher Rob Sanders has believed in and supported this project from its vaguest beginnings. The title is drawn from *Wood Mountain Poems* by Andrew Suknaski—"this is my right/to chronicle the meaning of these vast plains/in a geography of blood and failure/making them live"—and is used with his permission.

It only remains to express my gratitude for the beauty of the Cypress Hills, which stops us in our tracks and makes us listen.

{NOTES}

Notes refer to direct quotations only. Additional information on sources is provided in the bibliography.

CHAPTER 1: *Getting There*
1. G. K. Chesterton, *On Running After One's Hat and Other Whimsies* (New York: Robert M. McBride, 1935), 6.

CHAPTER 2: *The Stegner House*
1. Wallace Stegner, *Wolf Willow: A History, a Story, and a Memory of the Last Plains Frontier* (New York: Penguin Books, 2000), 5, 7.
2. Ibid., 277.
3. Ibid., 15–16.
4. Eastend History Society, *Range Riders and Sodbusters* (Eastend, SK: Eastend History Society, 1984), x.
5. Ibid., 662.
6. Ibid., 765.
7. Ibid., 771.

CHAPTER 3: *Digging In*
1. Wallace Stegner, *Wolf Willow,* 19.
2. Ibid., 18.
3. Chahiksichahiks (Pawnee) song, as quoted by Candace Savage, *Prairie: A Natural History* (Vancouver: Greystone Books, 2004), 16.

CHAPTER 4: *Ravenscrag Road*
1. Wallace Stegner, *Wolf Willow,* 283.
2. Ibid., 255.
3. Ibid., 297.
4. Ibid., 281.
5. Ibid., 300.
6. Ibid., 29–30.
7. Ibid., 73–74.
8. Ibid., 66.
9. Ibid., 56.
10. Ibid., 65.
11. Ibid., 61.
12. Ibid., 118.
13. Henry David Thoreau, *Walden Or, A Life in the Woods* (Boston: Houghton-Mifflin, 1897), 122.
14. Wallace Stegner, *Wolf Willow,* 24.
15. Ibid., 49–50.
16. Ibid., 53.
17. Ibid., 66.

CHAPTER 5: *Stone Circles*
1. Johannes Brahms, *Ein Deutsches Requiem,* 1868.
2. George Bird Grinnell, *The Punishment of the Stingy and Other Indian Stories* (New York: Harper and Brother, 1901), ix, x, 219–32. Accessed at http://www.sacred-texts.com.

CHAPTER 6: *Chimney Coulee*
1. Isaac Cowie, *The Company of Adventurers: A Narrative of Seven Years in the Service of the Hudson's Bay Company During 1867–1874, On the Great Buffalo Plains* (Lincoln: University of Nebraska Press, 1993), 436–37.
2. William Shakespeare, *The Tempest,* Act 1, Scene 2.
3. Unnamed speaker, quoted by Capt. W.F. Butler, *The Great Lone Land: A Narrative of Travel and Adventure in the North-West of America.* (London: Sampson Low, Marston, Low, and Searle, 1872), 362.
4. Isaac Cowie, *The Company of Adventurers,* 434.
5. Unnamed speaker, quoted by Capt. W.F. Butler, *The Great Lone Land,* 271.
6. Isaac Cowie, *The Company of Adventurers,* 435.
7. Wallace Stegner, *Wolf Willow,* 65.
8. Norbert Welsh, accessed on Nov. 10, 2010, at http://www.louisrielinstitute.com/culture/buffalohunt.php.

CHAPTER 7: *Modern Times*

1. Tour guide's commentary, re Cypress Hills massacre, based on remarks from our expert guide, Clayton Y. Yarshenko, and from his "Agenda Paper" and "Historical Context Address" on the same subject.
2. Montana press, as quoted by Beth LaDow, *The Medicine Line: Life and Death on a North American Borderland* (New York: Routledge, 2001), 31.
3. Richard Irving Dodge, *Our Wild Indians: Thirty-Three Years Personal Experience Among the Red Men* (Hartford: A.D. Worthington, 1882), 295.
4. Dodge, as quoted by Capt. W.F. Butler, *The Great Lone Land,* 241.
5. Unnamed "high-ranking officer," as quoted by David D. Smits, "The Frontier Army and the Destruction of the Buffalo," *Western Historical Quarterly* 25 (1994): 331.
6. Dan Kennedy (Ochankugahe), *Recollections of an Assiniboine Chief* (Toronto: McClelland and Stewart, 1972), 49–50.

CHAPTER 8: *Fort Walsh*

1. Sweet Bird (Misacongae), Report of the Commissioner, North-West Mounted Police, 1876, in Commissioners of the Royal North-West Mounted Police, *Opening Up the West: Being the Official Reports to Parliament of the Activities of the Royal North-West Mounted Police Force from 1874–1881* (Toronto: Coles, 1973), 38.
2. Report of the Sioux Commission, December 18, 1876, as quoted by Garrett Wilson, *Frontier Farewell: the 1870s and the End of the Old West* (Regina: Canadian Plains Research Centre, 2007), 287.
3. Sitting Bull, Report of the Commissioner, North-West Mounted Police, 1876, in *Opening Up the West,* 38.
4. General Terry, Report of the Sitting Bull Indian Commission (Washington, D.C., 1877), 7.
5. Sitting Bull, Report of the Sitting Bull Indian Commission, 8.
6. Commissioner James F. Macleod, Report of the Commissioner, North-West Mounted Police, 1877, 49, and Report of the Sitting Bull Indian Commission, 10.
7. Unnamed Aboriginal man, quoted in a letter from George McDougall to Alexander Morris, October 23, 1875, as cited by Hugh A. Dempsey, "The Fearsome Fire Wagon," in Hugh Dempsey, ed. *The CPR West: The Iron Road and the Making of a Nation* (Vancouver: Douglas & McIntyre, 1984), 56.
8. Treaty Commissioner Alexander Morris, *The Treaties of Canada with the Indians of Manitoba and the North-West Territories* (Toronto: Willing and Williamson, 1880), 92, 95, 98, 211.

9. Indian Affairs bureaucrat Colonel J.S. Dennis, in a letter to Edgar Dewdney, June 23, 1879, as quoted by Garrett Wilson, *Frontier Farewell*, 358.

10. Sir John A. Macdonald, from Edgar Dewdney papers, "Memo of My Appointment as Indian Commissioner, 1879," as quoted by Garrett Wilson, *Frontier Farewell*, 357.

11. Edgar Dewdney, from his journal, 1879, Glenbow Archives M-320-p.1039.

12. Colonel Macleod, as quoted by Edgar Dewdney, in Report of the Deputy Superintendent of Indian Affairs, 1879, 77. Accessed online at http://www.collectionscanada.gc.ca/databases/indianaffairs/.

13. Edgar Dewdney, from his journal, 1879, Glenbow Archives M-320-p.1039.

14. Ibid.

15. Mistahi-maskwa (Big Bear), from a letter from George McDougall to A. Morris, Oct. 23, 1875, as quoted by Hugh A. Dempsey, *Big Bear: The End of Freedom* (Vancouver: Douglas & McIntyre, 1984), 63.

16. Edgar Dewdney, in Report of the Deputy Superintendent of Indian Affairs, 1879, 77.

17. Ibid.

CHAPTER 9: *The Hunger Camp*

1. Sir John A. Macdonald, Report of the Department of Indian Affairs for the Year Ended 31st December 1881, 7. Accessed online at http://www.collectionscanada.gc.ca/databases/indianaffairs/.

2. Thunder Child, as recorded by Rev. Edward Ahenakew and quoted by Hugh A. Dempsey, *Big Bear: The End of Freedom*, 101–102.

3. Official correspondence, June 13, 1881, RG10 C-10131 volume 3745 file 29506-1.

4. Edgar Dewdney to head office, July 16, 1881, RG10 C-10131 volume 3745 file 29506-1.

5. Edgar Dewdney, Report of the Department of Indian Affairs for the Year Ended 31st December 1883. Accessed online at http://www.collectionscanada.gc.ca/databases/indianaffairs/.

6. Edgar Dewdney, letter to Lt. Col. Irvine, Fort Walsh, Oct. 27, 1882, RG10 C-10131 volume 3744 file 29506-2.

7. Indian Agent Denny to head office, Dec. 1881, RG10 C-10131 volume 3745 file 29506-1.

8. Indian Agent McIlree (successor to Denny) to his superiors, Dec. 2, 1882, RG10 C-10131 volume 3744 file 29506-3.

9. Ibid.

10. Fred R. White to Edgar Dewdney, Oct. 17, 1882, RG10 C-10131 volume 3744 file 29506-2.
11. Augustus Jukes to Edgar Dewdney, Oct. 21, 1882, RG10 C-10134 volume 3744 file 29506-2.
12. Edgar Dewdney to Sir John A. Macdonald, Oct. 21, 1882, RG10 C-10131 volume 3744 file 29506-2.
13. Edgar Dewdney to Lt. Col. French, Oct. 27, 1882, RG10 C-10131 volume 3744 file 29506-2.
14. Indian Agent A. Macdonald to Edgar Dewdney, Nov. 11, 1882, RG10 C-10131 volume 3744 file 29506-3.

CHAPTER 10: *Creation Stories*
1. Gordon Oakes, *Statement of Treaty Issues: Treaties as a Bridge to the Future* (n.p.: Office of the Treaty Commissioner, 1998), 68.
2. Letter from Front Man to the Minister of Indians, summer 1897, RG10 C-12061 volume 7779 file 27140.
3. Correspondence, July 3, 1881, RG10 C-10131 volume 3745 file 29506-1.
4. Nekaneet as quoted by W.W.F., Special Correspondent, "Indian Grievances. An Interesting Talk With One of Pie-a-Pot's Head Men." *Daily Mail,* Toronto, April 24, 1885, p. 1 ff.
5. Maureen K. Lux, *Medicine That Walks: Disease, Medicine, and Canadian Plains Native People, 1880–1940* (Toronto: University of Toronto Press, 2002).
6. Petition signed by Stoney Indian, Oct. 24, 1914, RG10 C-10131 volume 3744 file 29506-3.
7. Wallace Stegner, *Wolf Willow,* 49–50.

CHAPTER 11: *Home Truth*
1. Sir John A. Macdonald to Edgar Dewdney, Nov. 20, 1885, as quoted by Blair Stonechild and Bill Waiser, *Loyal Till Death: Indians and the North-West Rebellion* (Calgary: Fifth House, 1997), 221.
2. W.W.F., Special Correspondent, "Indian Grievances. An Interesting Talk With One of Pie-a-Pot's Head Men." *Daily Mail,* Toronto, April 24, 1885, p. 1 ff.

{BIBLIOGRAPHY}

FOR FURTHER READING

Ahenakew, Edward. *Voices of the Plains Cree.* Toronto: McClelland
    and Stewart, 1973.

Butala, Sharon. *The Perfection of the Morning: An Apprenticeship in Nature.*
    Toronto: HarperCollins, 1994.

Butler, Capt. W.F. *The Great Lone Land: A Narrative of Travel and Adventure
    in the North-West of America.* London: Sampson Low, Marston, Low,
    and Searle, 1872.

Gibson, Ross. *Seven Versions of an Australian Badland.* St. Lucia: University
    of Queensland Press, 2002.

Herriot, Trevor. *River in a Dry Land: A Prairie Passage.* Toronto: Stoddard,
    2000.

Kennedy, Dan (Ochankugahe). *Recollections of an Assiniboine Chief.*
    Toronto: McClelland and Stewart, 1972.

Klar, Barbara. *Cypress.* London: Brick Books, 2008.

Sandoz, Mari. *The Buffalo Hunters.* New York: Hastings House, 1954.

Stegner, Wallace. *Wolf Willow: A History, a Story, and a Memory of the
    Last Plains Frontier.* 1962. New York: Penguin, 2000.

Suknaski, Andrew. *Wood Mountain Poems.* 1976. Region: Hagios, 2006.

Vanderhaeghe, Guy. *The Englishman's Boy.* Toronto: McClelland and
    Stewart, 1996.

——. *The Last Crossing.* Toronto: McClelland and Stewart, 2002.

——. *A Good Man.* Toronto: McClelland and Stewart, 2011.

CHAPTER 1: *Getting There*

Bonnichsen, Robson, and Stuart J. Baldwin, *Cypress Hills Ethnohistory and Ecology: A Regional Perspective.* Archaeological Survey of Alberta Occasional Paper no. 10, 1978.

Dickinson, Dawn M., David A. Gauthier, and Bob Mutch, eds. *Proceedings of the Cypress Hills Forest Management Workshop.* Medicine Hat: Medicine Hat College, 1992.

Eggleston, Wilfrid. "The Cypress Hills," *Canadian Geographical Journal* 62 (February 1951): 52–67.

Hildebrandt, Walter, and Brian Hubner. *The Cypress Hills: An Island by Itself.* Saskatoon: Purich, 2007.

McVeigh, Stephen. *The American Western.* Edinburgh: Edinburgh University Press, 2007.

Potter, James E. "Epilogue: The Pageant Revisited: Indian Wars Medal of Honor In Nebraska, 1865–1879." In *The Nebraska Indian Wars Reader,* edited by R. Eli Paul, pp. 217–30. Lincoln: University of Nebraska Press, 1998.

Savage, Candace. *Cowgirls.* Vancouver: Douglas & McIntyre, 1996.

Warren, Louis S. *Buffalo Bill's America: William Cody and the Wild West Show.* New York: Alfred A. Knopf, 2005.

Zell, R.L., ed. Cypress Hills Plateau, Alberta and Saskatchewan. *Guidebook, Part 1. Fifteenth Annual Field Conference,* Alberta Society of Petroleum Geologists, 1965.

CHAPTER 2: *The Stegner House*

This chapter is informed, in part, by conversations with writer Seán Virgo, Eastend.

Eastend History Society, *Range Riders and Sodbusters.* Eastend, SK: Eastend History Society, 1984.

Stegner, Wallace. *Wolf Willow: A History, A Story, and a Memory of the Last Plains Frontier.* 1962. New York: Penguin, 2000.

CHAPTER 3: *Digging In*

This chapter is informed by conversations with Tim Tokaryk, T.rex Discovery Centre and Royal Saskatchewan Museum.

Bell, Sean D. "Aplodontid, Sciurid, Castorid, Zapodid and Geomyoid Rodents of the Rodent Hill Locality, Cypress Hills Formation, Southwest, Saskatchewan." M.Sc. thesis, University of Saskatchewan, 2004.

Fox, R.C., "The Oldest Cenozoic Mammal?" *Journal of Vertebrate Paleontology* 22 (June 2002): 456–69.

Kehoe, Thomas F. *The Gull Lake Site: A Prehistoric Bison Drive Site in Southwestern Saskatchewan.* Milwaukee Public Museum Publications in Anthropology and History. Number 1, 1973.

McKenzie-McAnally, L., ed. "Upper Cretaceous and Tertiary Stratigraphy and Paleontology of Southern Saskatchewan." *Canadian Paleontology Conference Field Trip Guidebook,* Number 6, 1997.

Olson, Wes. *Portraits of the Bison: An Illustrated Guide to Bison Society.* Edmonton: University of Alberta Press, 2005.

Savage, Candace. *Prairie: A Natural History.* 2004. Vancouver: Douglas & McIntyre, 2011.

Stegner, Wallace. *Wolf Willow: A History, a Story, and a Memory of the Last Plains Frontier.* 1962. New York: Penguin, 2000.

Storer, John E. "Eocene-Oligocene Faunas of the Cypress Hills Formation, Saskatchewan." In *The Terrestrial Eocene-Oligocene Transition in North America,* edited by Donald R. Prothero and Robert J. Emry, pp. 240–61. Cambridge: Cambridge University Press, 1998.

Tokaryk, Tim T., and Harold N. Bryant. "The Fauna from the *Tyrannosaurus rex* Excavation, Frenchman Formation (Late Maastrichtian) Saskatchewan." In *Summary of Investigations,* volume 1, Saskatchewan Geological Survey, Sask. Industry Resources, Mis. Rep. 2004-4.1, CD-ROM Paper A-18.

CHAPTER 4: *Ravenscrag Road*

This chapter is informed, in part, by conversations with Dr. David Sauchyn, University of Regina.

Cook-Lynn, Elizabeth. *Why I Can't Read Wallace Stegner and Other Essays: A Tribal Voice.* Madison: University of Wisconsin Press, 1996.

Ravenscrag History Book Committee. *Between and Beyond the Benches: Ravenscrag.* Edited by Ann Saville. Ravenscrag: Ravenscrag History Book Committee, 1981.

Stegner, Wallace. *Wolf Willow: A History, a Story, and a Memory of the Last Plains Frontier.* 1962. New York: Penguin, 2000.

Storer, John E. *Geological History of Saskatchewan.* Regina: Saskatchewan Museum of Natural History, 1989.

Zell, R.L., ed. Cypress Hills Plateau, Alberta and Saskatchewan. *Guidebook, Part 1. Fifteenth Annual Field Conference,* Alberta Society of Petroleum Geologists, 1965.

CHAPTER 5: *Stone Circles*

This chapter is informed, in part, by conversations with Dr. David Meyer, University of Saskatchewan; Dr. Gerald Oetelaar and Dr. Brian Reeves, University of Calgary; and Dr. Alison Landals, Stantec Consulting.

Berry, Susan, and Jack Brink. *Aboriginal Cultures in Alberta: Five Hundred Generations.* Edmonton: Royal Alberta Museum, 2005.

Brink, Jack W., and J.F. Dormaar., eds. *Archaeology in Alberta: A View From the New Millennium.* Medicine Hat: Archaeological Society of Alberta, 2003.

Bryan, Liz. *The Buffalo People: Prehistoric Archaeology on the Canadian Plains.* Edmonton: University of Alberta Press, 1991.

Epp, Henry, and Ian Dyck. "Early Human-Bison Population Interdependence in the Plains Ecosystem." *Great Plains Research* 12 (fall 2002): 323–37.

Grinnell, George Bird. "Little Friend Coyote." In *The Punishment of the Stingy and Other Indian Stories,* pp. 219–32. New York: Harper and Brother, 1901. Accessed at http://www.sacred-texts.com.

Kooyman, Brian, and Jane H. Kelley, eds. *Archaeology on the Edge: New Perspectives from the Northern Plains.* Calgary: University of Calgary Press, 2004.

Morin, Jean-Pierre. "Empty Hills: Aboriginal Land Usage and the Cypress Hills Problem." *Saskatchewan History* 55 (spring 2003): 5–20.

Reeves, Brian O.K. "Communal Bison Hunters of the Northern Plains." In *Hunters of the Recent Past,* edited by Leslie B. Davis and Brian O.K. Reeves, pp. 168–94. London: Unwin Hyman, 1990.

CHAPTER 6: *Chimney Coulee*

Binnema, Theodore. *Common and Contested Ground: A Human and Environmental History of the Northwestern Plains.* Toronto: University of Toronto Press, 2004.

Burley, David V. "Function, Meaning and Context: Ambiguities in Ceramic Use by the *Hivernant* Metis of the Northwestern Plains." *Historical Archaeology* 23, no. 1 (1989): 97–106.

Burley, David V., Gayel A. Horsfall, and John D. Brandon. *Structural Considerations of Métis Ethnicity: An Archaeological, Architectural, and Historical Study.* Vermilion: University of South Dakota Press, 1992.

Butler, Capt. W.F. *The Great Lone Land: A Narrative of Travel and Adventure in the North-West of America.* London: Sampson Low, Marston, Low, and Searle, 1872.

Cowie, Isaac. *The Company of Adventurers: A Narrative of Seven Years in the Service of the Hudson's Bay Company During 1867–1874, On the Great Buffalo Plains.* 1913. Lincoln: University of Nebraska Press, 1993.

Dobak, William A. "Killing the Canadian Buffalo, 1821–1881." In *Canadian Environmental History: Essential Readings,* edited by David Freeland Duke, pp. 239–57. Toronto: Canadian Scholars Press, 2006.

Elliott, Jack. "Hivernant Archaeology in the Cypress Hills." M.A. thesis, University of Calgary, 1971.

Foster, Martha Harroun. "'Just Following the Buffalo,' Origins of a Montana Métis Community." *Great Plains Quarterly* 26 (summer 2006): 185–202.

Isenberg, Andrew C. *The Destruction of the Bison: An Environmental History, 1750–1920.* Cambridge: Cambridge University Press, 2000.

Kennedy, Margaret. "West Block Cypress Hills, Archaeological Inventory 1995, Permit #95-48." Department of Anthropology and Archaeology, University of Saskatchewan, Saskatoon. 1997.

Milloy, John S. *The Plains Cree: Trade, Diplomacy and War, 1790 to 1870.* Winnipeg: University of Manitoba Press, 1988.

Nelson, J.G. *The Last Refuge.* Montreal: Harvest House, 1973.

Oetelaar, Gerald A. "Tipi Rings and Alberta Archaeology: A Brief Overview." In *Archaeology in Alberta: A View From the New Millennium,* edited by Jack W. Brink and John F. Dormaar, pp. 104–30. Medicine Hat: Archaeological Society of Alberta, 2003.

Sentar Consultants [John D. Brandon]. Archaeology at Chimney Coulee (1994) Permit #94-72, prepared for Eastend Community Tourism Authority, 1995.

Stegner, Wallace. *Wolf Willow: A History, a Story, and a Memory of the Last Plains Frontier.* 1962. New York: Penguin, 2000.

Welsh Norbert, as told to Mary Weekes. *The Last Buffalo Hunter.* New York: Thomas Nelson, 1939.

CHAPTER 7: *Modern Times*

This chapter is based, in part, on presentations by Val Ryder of the Carry the Kettle First Nation at History in the Hills, June 2006.

Dempsey, Hugh A. "Cypress Hills Massacre." *Montana: Magazine of History* 3 (autumn 1953): 1–9.

Dodge, Richard Irving. *Our Wild Indians: Thirty-Three Years of Personal Experience Among the Red Men.* Hartford: A.D. Worthington, 1882.

Goldring, P. "The Cypress Hills Massacre—A Century's Retrospect."
   Saskatchewan History 26 (autumn 1973): 81–102.

Hildebrandt, Walter, and Brian Hubner. *The Cypress Hills: An Island by Itself.*
   Saskatoon: Purich, 2007.

Indian Claims Commission. "Carry the Kettle First Nation Inquiry
   Cypress Hills Claim," July 2000.

Isenberg, Andrew C. *The Destruction of the Bison: An Environmental History,
   1750–1920.* Cambridge: Cambridge University Press, 2000.

Kennedy, Dan (Ochankugahe). *Recollections of an Assiniboine Chief.*
   Toronto: McClelland and Stewart, 1972.

Kennedy, Margaret A. *The Whiskey Trade of the Northwestern Plains:
   A Multidisciplinary Study.* New York: P. Lang, 1997.

LaDow, Beth. *The Medicine Line: Life and Death on a North American
   Borderland.* New York: Routledge, 2001.

Sharp, Paul. *Whoop-Up Country: The Canadian-American West, 1865–1885.*
   Norman: University of Oklahoma Press, 1973.

Smits, David D. "The Frontier Army and the Destruction of the Buffalo."
   Western Historical Quarterly 25 (autumn 1994): 313–38.

Yarshenko, Clayton Y. "Agenda Paper: The Cypress Hills Massacre."
   Historic Sites and Monuments Board of Canada, n.d.

——. "Historical Context Address." S.W. Saskatchewan Oldtimers
   Association Museum and Archives, June 20, 1998.

CHAPTER 8: *Fort Walsh*

*This chapter is based, in part, on conversations with Dr. Margaret Kennedy,
   University of Saskatchewan, and with Royce Pettijohn, and Clayton
   Y. Yarshenko of Fort Walsh National Historic Site and the Southwest
   Saskatchewan Oldtimers Association.*

Commissioners of the Royal North-West Mounted Police. *Opening Up the
   West: Being the Official Reports to Parliament of the Activities of the Royal
   North-West Mounted Police Force From 1874–1881.* Toronto: Coles, 1973.

Cooney, C.J. "The Artful Dewdney: New Light on the Sketchy Character of
   the Honourable Edgar Dewdney." *British Columbia History* 42 (2009):
   11–17.

Dempsey, Hugh A. *Big Bear: The End of Freedom.* Lincoln: University of
   Nebraska Press, 1984.

——. "The Fearsome Fire Wagon." In *The CPR West: The Iron Road and the
   Making of a Nation,* edited by Hugh A. Dempsey, pp. 55–69. Vancouver:
   Douglas & McIntyre, 1984.

Denny, Sir Cecil E. *Denny's Trek: A Mountie's Memoir of the March West.* Victoria: Heritage House, 2005.

Dewdney, Edgar. Journal, 1879. Glenbow Archives M-320-p.1039.

Dodson, Peter. *Little Pine and Lucky Man; A History 1866–85.* Saskatoon: Office of the Treaty Commissioner, 2003.

Indian Affairs Annual Reports, 1864–1990, Library and Archives of Canada, http://www.collectionscanada.gc.ca/databases/indianaffairs/.

McCullough, A.B. "Papers Relating to the North-West Mounted Police and Fort Walsh," Research paper for Parks Canada, 1977.

Morris, Alexander. *The Treaties of Canada with the Indians of Manitoba and the North-West Territories.* Toronto: Willing and Williamson, 1880.

Public Archives of Canada. Record Group 10. (Papers of the Department of Indian Affairs and Northern Development and its predecessors, accessed on microfilm at the University of Saskatchewan.)

Report of the Sitting Bull Indian Commission. Washington: Government Printing Office, 1877.

Titley, Brian. *The Frontier World of Edgar Dewdney.* Vancouver: UBC Press, 1999.

Treaty 7 Elders and Tribal Council, et al. *The True Spirit and Original Intent of Treaty 7.* London, ON: McGill-Queen's University Press, 1996.

Turner, John Peter. *The North-West Mounted Police.* 2 vols. Ottawa: Edmond Cloutier, 1950.

Wilson, Garrett. *Frontier Farewell: The 1870s and the End of the Old West.* Regina: Canadian Plains Research Center, 2007.

Yarshenko, Clayton Y. "The Real Story of the Great March West: Ground to a Halt." Article written for Parks Canada, n.p., n.d.

CHAPTER 9: *The Hunger Camp*

This chapter is based, in part, on conversations with the late John Tobias.

Carter, Sarah. *Aboriginal People and Colonizers of Western Canada to 1900.* Toronto: University of Toronto Press, 1999.

——. *Lost Harvests: Prairie Indian Reserve Farmers and Government Policy.* Montreal: McGill-Queen's University Press, 1990.

Commissioners of the Royal North-West Mounted Police. *Opening Up the West: Being the Official Reports to Parliament of the Activities of the Royal North-West Mounted Police Force From 1874–1881.* Toronto: Coles, 1973.

——. *Settlers and Rebels: Being the Official Reports to Parliament of the Activities of the Royal North-West Mounted Police Force From 1882–1885.* Toronto: Coles, 1973.

Dawson, George M. "Big Bear's (Cree) Camp, Maple Creek, Saskatchewan. June 6, 1883." Photograph, Public Archives of Canada PA-050746.

Dempsey, Hugh A. *Big Bear: The End of Freedom.* Lincoln: University of Nebraska Press, 1984.

Hogue, Michel. *Crossing the Line: The Plains Cree in the Canada–United States Borderlands, 1870–1900.* M.A. Thesis, Department of History, University of Calgary, 2002.

——. "Disputing the Medicine Line: The Plains Crees and the Canadian-American Border, 1876–1885." *Montana: the Magazine of Western History* 52 (winter 2002): 2–17.

Indian Affairs Annual Reports, 1864–1990, Library and Archives of Canada, http://www.collectionscanada.gc.ca/databases/ indianaffairs/.

Little Bear, Isabelle. "My Own Story. Isabelle Little Bear One of Last Remaining Links With Riel Rebellion." *Bonnyville Tribune,* April 18, April 25, and May 2, 1958.

Public Archives of Canada. Record Group 10. (Papers of the Department of Indian Affairs and Northern Development and its predecessors, accessed on microfilm at the University of Saskatchewan.)

Tobias, John L. "Canada's Subjugation of the Plains Creek, 1879–1885." *Canadian Historical Review* 64 (1983): 519–48.

Wilson, Garrett. *Frontier Farewell: The 1870s and the End of the Old West.* Regina: Canadian Plains Research Center, 2007.

CHAPTER 10: *Creation Stories*
This chapter is informed by conversations with Harry Francis, Dale Mosquito, Linda Oakes, then-Chief Alice Pahtayken, the members of the oral-history classes at the Okimaw Ohci Healing Lodge (2010 and 2011), and, especially, Jean Francis Oakes.

Basso, Keith H. *Wisdom Sits in Places: Landscape and Language among the Western Apache.* Albuquerque: University of New Mexico Press, 1996.

Braroe, Niels Winther. "Kinds of Plains Cree Culture." *Ethnology* 41 (summer 2002): 263–80.

——. *Indian and White: Self-Image and Interaction in a Canadian Plains Community.* Stanford: Stanford University Press, 1975.

Hardeman, Nicholas P. "Brick Stronghold of the Border: Fort Assinniboine, 1879–1911." *Montana: Magazine of Western History* 29 (spring 1979): 54–67.

Hogue, Michel. *Crossing the Line: The Plains Cree in the Canada–United States Borderlands, 1870–1900.* M.A. Thesis, Department of History, University of Calgary, 2002.

Lee David. "Foremost Man, and His Band." *Saskatchewan History* 36 (1983): 94–101.

Lux, Maureen K. *Medicine That Walks: Disease, Medicine, and Canadian Plains Native People, 1880–1940.* Toronto: University of Toronto Press, 2002.

Oakes, Jean Francis. *Stories From My Life.* Privately published, 2008.

Public Archives of Canada. Record Group 10. (Papers of the Department of Indian Affairs and Northern Development and its predecessors, accessed on microfilm at the University of Saskatchewan.)

Statement of Treaty Issues: Treaties as a Bridge to the Future. Saskatoon: Office of the Treaty Commissioner, 1998.

Stegner, Wallace. *Wolf Willow: A History, a Story, and a Memory of the Last Plains Frontier.* 1962. New York: Penguin, 2000.

Watetch, Abel, as told to Blodwen Davies. *Payepot and His People.* Regina: Saskatchewan History and Folklore Society, 1959.

W.W.F., Special Correspondent. "Indian Grievances. An Interesting Talk With One of Pie-a-Pot's Head Men." *Daily Mail,* Toronto (April 24, 1885): 1 ff.

CHAPTER 11: *Home Truth*

This chapter is informed by conversations with the late Curly Bear Wagner of the Going to the Sun Institute, Narcisse Blood of Red Crow College, and Nora Hassell.

Chambers, Cynthia M., and Narcisse J. Blood. "Love Thy Neighbour: Repatriating Precarious Blackfoot Sites." http://www.learnalberta.ca/content/ssmc/html/lovethyneighbor_aStory.html.

Gulliford, Andrew. *Sacred Objects and Sacred Places: Preserving Tribal Traditions.* Boulder: University Press of Colorado, 2000.

In the Light of Reverence, produced by Christopher McLeod and Malinda Maynor (Sacred Land Film Project, Earth Island Institute, 2001).

Oetelaar, Gerald A., and D. Joy Oetelaar. "People, Places and Paths: The Cypress Hills and the Nitsitapii Landscape of Southern Alberta." *Plains Archaeologist* 51 (2006): 375–97.

Savage, Candace. "Eight Thousand Years Down." *Canadian Geographic* (Nov./Dec. 2006) http://www.canadiangeographic.ca/magazine/nd06/feature_8000.asp.

Stonechild, Blair and Bill Waiser. *Loyal Till Death: Indians and the North-West Rebellion.* Calgary: Fifth House, 1997.

Sundstrom, Linea. "Sacred Islands: Exploration of Religion and Landscape in the Northern Great Plains." In *Islands on the Plains: Ecological, Social, and Ritual Use of Landscapes,* edited by Marcel Kornfeld and Alan J. Osborn, pp. 258–300. Salt Lake City: University of Utah Press, 2003.

{INDEX}

{THE DAVID SUZUKI FOUNDATION}

THE David Suzuki Foundation works through science and education to protect the diversity of nature and our quality of life, now and for the future.

With a goal of achieving sustainability within a generation, the Foundation collaborates with scientists, business and industry, academia, government and non-governmental organizations. We seek the best research to provide innovative solutions that will help build a clean, competitive economy that does not threaten the natural services that support all life.

The Foundation is a federally registered independent charity that is supported with the help of over 50,000 individual donors across Canada and around the world.

We invite you to become a member. For more information on how you can support our work, please contact us:

The David Suzuki Foundation
219–2211 West 4th Avenue
Vancouver, BC
Canada V6K 4S2
www.davidsuzuki.org
contact@davidsuzuki.org
Tel: 604-732-4228
Fax: 604-732-0752

Checks can be made payable to the David Suzuki Foundation.
All donations are tax-deductible.

Canadian charitable registration: (BN) 12775 6716 RR0001

U.S. charitable registration: #94-3204049